THE BIRTH OF A NATION

'In the eighteenth century the world was becoming one world but

Australia was still a world of its own.' GEOFFREY BLAINEY

'You are to proceed to the southward in order to make discovery of the Continent above-mentioned . . .'

COOK'S SEALED ORDERS, 1768

one Deep'd 240lb exclusive of th[e]

In the Am as the Wind still contin[ued]
I sent the Yawl again afishin[g]
With a party of Men into the Coun[try]
With nothing extraordinary —

Sunday 6th In the evening th[e]
from fishing having caught two
Dugong near 600 pound[s]
~~the one weigh'd~~ ~~present and th[e]~~

~~exclusive of the entrails~~ The gre[at]
~~rof~~ Plants &c. Mr Banks & Dr Solande[r]
~~of these~~ ~~lot~~ ~~fifty~~ ~~found~~ in th[e]
occasioned my giving it the
Botany Bay . . .
~~Bay Harbour~~ it is situated i[n]
of 34° 0' S Longitude 208° 37' We[st]
safe and commodious. it may be kno[wn]
                                    is of a prettyeven and moder[ate]
on the sea coast which is ~~level~~ and
that it is fav'ring . . .

entrails —

...d northerly
...and 9 dent
...y but not

...Yawl returnd
...ting rag,
...other

...quantity
...collecte
...place
...me of
...the Latitude
...it is Capacious
...by the land
...high
...there...

...bing within that Island
7, 6 and five fathom a go...
a good way off from th...
point quite to the head...
the north and N W sho...
at low water
Dater, 3 or 4 leagues up...
~~but there~~ *but there I*
anchord near the sout...
entrance for the conv...
Dind and the getting off...
a very __fine__ *stream of...*
in the first sandy cove...
adry
night lay almost land...
every where: altho woo...
is very little variety
and grow
than our oaks in len...
it self is heavy, hard a...

THE BIRTH OF A NATION

Australia's Historic Heritage
from Discovery to Nationhood

With Contributions by
Geoffrey Blainey, Michael Cannon, Alan Moorehead
John Ritchie, R. M. Younger, John Currey

ROBIN SMITH

VIKING O'NEIL

Viking O'Neil
Penguin Books Australia Ltd
487 Maroondah Highway, PO Box 257
Ringwood, Victoria 3134, Australia
Penguin Books Ltd
Harmondsworth, Middlesex, England
Penguin Books
40 West 23rd Street, New York, N.Y. 10010, U.S.A.
Penguin Books Canada Limited
2801 John Street, Markham, Ontario, Canada L3R 1B4
Penguin Books (N.Z.) Ltd
182-190 Wairau Road, Auckland 10, New Zealand

First published by John Currey, O'Neil Pty Ltd 1978
as *The Birth of Australia*
Published as *Australia's Historic Heritage* 1981
This edition published by Penguin Books Australia Ltd 1987
Copyright © Photographs: Robin Smith, 1978

Produced by Viking O'Neil
56 Claremont Street, South Yarra, Victoria 3141, Australia,
a division of Penguin Books Australia Ltd

Typeset in 12 point Garamond
Printed and bound in Hong Kong through Bookbuilders Ltd

National Library of Australia
Cataloguing-in-Publication data

Smith, Robin (Robin Vaughan Francis).
    The birth of a nation.

ISBN 0 670 90018 4.

1. Historic buildings — Australia — Pictorial works.
2. Architecture — Australia — Pictorial works. I.
Blainey, Geoffrey, 1930-   . II. Smith, Robin (Robin
Vaughan Francis). Australia's historic heritage.
III. Title.

720'.994

Previous pages show:
pp 2-3 Cooktown, Queensland
pp 4-5 H M Bark *Endeavour*, scale replica
by Bruce and Ross Usher, Sydney
pp 6-7 James Cook's *Endeavour* journal in
the National Library of Australia, Canberra

Acknowledgements

This book has been many years in the making and is the product of literally thousands of kilometres' travelling across the continent. It would not be feasible to attempt to thank all the people who have assisted in its making, for there are so many of them: administrators of museums and historic buildings; members of local historical societies; librarians; public authorities and Australians who find themselves by an accident of fate or family entrusted with a part of the National Estate. Their reward is the thanks of a grateful public. I would like to record, however, that without the support, assistance and understanding of Maggy Oehlbeck, the book would not have been possible.

Photography The following organizations provided valuable assistance in the photography of properties or artefacts which they own or hold in trust: The Anglican Diocese of Sydney; The National Library of Australia, Canberra; Old Sydney Town Pty Ltd; The Mitchell Library, Sydney; The National Trust of New South Wales; The Department of Defence; The Department of Science; The New South Wales Department of Education; Port Arthur Settlement; The National Trust of Australia (Tasmania); Gippsland Folk Museum, Moe, Victoria; The Earlystreet Historical Village, Brisbane; Swan Hill Pioneer Settlement Authority; The National Trust of Australia (Victoria); The National Trust of South Australia; Beltana Pastoral Company Limited; ANZ Banking Group Limited; The National Trust of Australia (Western Australia); Western Mining Corporation; Gold Mines of Kalgoorlie; Broken Hill City Council; The National Trust of Queensland; The State Library of New South Wales; Somerville House, Brisbane High School for Girls; Home Missions Committee, Churches of Christ in Queensland.

The Ballarat East goldfields were photographed with the assistance of Tim Hobson, Curator of History, Sovereign Hill Gold Mining Township, Ballarat. Photography of the interior of public buildings and of historic documents was made possible by the permission of Sir Billy Snedden, Speaker of the House of Representatives; The Chief Justice of Victoria and the Speaker of the Legislative Assembly, Parliament of Victoria. My thanks are also due to Bruce and Ross Usher (*Endeavour*); Hedley and Jan Elliott ('Emu Bottom'); the Birbeck family ('Glenmore'); Mrs W F Archer ('Brickendon'); Mr and Mrs J H A Warner ('Valleyfield'); Mr Peter Muller ('Glenrock'); Mr and Mrs Quentin Stanham ('Camden Park'); Mr Royal ('Bedervale'); Mr Maiden ('Menindie'); Sir Richard Hawker ('Bungaree'); Mr and Mrs D Fellows ('Gulf Station'); Mr R G Holloway ('Tyntynder Station'); Mr Frank Cook ('Para Para'); Mr and Mrs M Hill-Smith ('Yalumba'); Stanley Hancock ('Eulalia'); Henry Scott and Neil Speed (Eureka), and John Swinfield.

R S

Text The publishers gratefully acknowledge the permission of authors, their agents and publishers to reproduce copyright material condensed from the following sources: pp 16-17: *The Tyranny of Distance* by Geoffrey Blainey, published by Sun Books and the Macmillan Company of Australia Pty Ltd; pp 42-45: *Australia: as once we were* by John Ritchie, published by William Heinemann Australia Pty Ltd; pp 66-69: *Australia! Australia! The Pioneer Years* by R M Younger, published by Rigby Limited; pp 100-103: *The Rush That Never Ended* by Geoffrey Blainey, published by Melbourne University Press; pp 140-143: *Cooper's Creek* by Alan Moorehead, published by Hamish Hamilton Limited; pp 156-159: *Australia in the Victorian Age: Life in the Country* by Michael Cannon, published by Thomas Nelson Australia Pty Ltd; pp 190-193: *Australia! Australia! March to Nationhood* by R M Younger, published by Rigby Limited.

Many of the organizations and individuals listed above also provided accurate information for the captions, which were prepared by the publisher's staff. Major additional sources were the publications of regional historical societies, state tourist authorities and the Australian Council of National Trusts. Particular thanks are due to Tim Hobson, Curator of History at Sovereign Hill Historical Park, Ballarat, and Stanley Hancock, President of the National Trust of Queensland, both of whom provided detailed and specific information for a number of photographs.

Contents

1 Discoverers GEOFFREY BLAINEY 14

Dutch navigators sail east from the Cape of Good Hope; the west coast discovered; Cook's voyage on the Endeavour, *1768*

2 Birthplace JOHN CURREY 20

Arthur Phillip sails with the First Fleet; rejects Cook's site at Botany Bay; discovers Port Jackson; the settlement faces crisis

3 Convicts JOHN RITCHIE 40

Transportation to the Australian penal colonies; the crimes of the convicts; how they were treated; preparing a new world

4 Settlers R M YOUNGER 64

Opening up the colonial grasslands; the lives of the early squatters; homes of wood, mud and bark fashioned from the bushland

5 Goldrush GEOFFREY BLAINEY 98

Edward Hammond Hargraves' shrewd publicity; the rush begins to Ophir; on the Victorian diggings; Eureka; after the rushes

6 Explorers ALAN MOOREHEAD 138

Sturt explores the rivers; his inland expeditions in search of the 'great inland sea'; the tragedy of Burke and Wills

7 On The Land MICHAEL CANNON 154

The selectors follow in the squatters' footsteps; their hardships; the 'wool kings' build their homesteads; rural life

8 Nationhood R M YOUNGER 188

Federation of the colonies; Queen Victoria's proclamation; celebrations; the first parliament; an Indian Summer

Left: More than 150 years before James Cook sighted the east coast of Australia, a Dutchman had landed on the west. Late in 1616 the Dutch East Indiaman *Eendracht* was taking the new route from South Africa to Java when she was carried east by the prevailing wind and, on 25 October, made landfall near the entrance of Shark Bay on the north-west coast of Western Australia. There, at Cape Inscription on present-day Dirk Hartog Island, the *Eendracht's* commander recorded his visit by inscribing a pewter plate which he fixed to a post before resuming his journey: 'On 25th October there arrived here the ship Eendraght of Amsterdam. Supercargo Gilles Miebais of Liege; skipper Dirck Hatichs of Amsterdam. On 27th do. she set sail again for Bantam . . .' The land he had seen was later shown on Dutch maps as Eendracht Land.

Discoverers

'At daylight on 20 April 1770, after running before a southerly gale, he saw sloping, timbered hills in the distance . . .'
GEOFFREY BLAINEY, *The Tyranny of Distance*

In the eighteenth century the world was becoming one world but Australia was still a world of its own. It was untouched by Europe's customs and commerce. It was more isolated than the Himalayas or the heart of Siberia. Each year hundreds of ships, like birds, glided from Europe to hotter lands to fill themselves with food and materials which Europe could not produce. As late as the eighteenth century, however, they shunned Australia. That land seemed to grow no bush or flower or grain which Europe wanted. It seemed to yield no precious metal or mineral. It produced no animal or fish for which European markets were willing to risk their ships in long voyages.

Dutchmen had sailed along much of Australia's coast, alert merchants and piercing-eyed navigators who saw nothing which pleased them. Ever since 1616 Dutch convoys had followed the route charted crudely and devised brilliantly by Hendrick Brouwer of the United East India Company of the Netherlands, who discovered that the quickest route on the outward voyage from Holland to Java was to sail east from the Cape of Good Hope for about 4800 kilometres and then steer north to Java. In sailing east from the tip of South Africa the ships harnessed the strength of the westerly winds on the fringes of the Roaring Forties and usually made swift passages to the vicinity of the western coast of Australia, where they changed course and sailed north towards Java.

Some ships bound for Java strayed too far south and east and when they changed course for the run up to Java found a long barren coast blocking their passage; in 1627 a Dutch ship sailed a thousand miles along the southern coast of Australia and was 500 sea miles from the site of what is now the city of Adelaide before she retreated. Other Dutchmen crossing the Indian Ocean in warmer latitudes were blown too far to the east and saw the western coast of Australia.

As Australia's west coast flanked one of the world's richest and loneliest trade routes, it was seen and visited at countless points by Dutch ships passing on their way from Europe or by a few Dutch ships which were sent from Djakarta in search of new lands and riches. The first Dutch commercial fleet had reached the East Indies in 1596 — eight years after the year of the Great Armada — and in the following half century Abel Tasman and Dutchmen had traced nearly two-thirds of Australia's coastline.

More than a century and a half passed from the day when the first European sailors saw Australia's west coast to the day when the first European sailors saw the east coast or the hidden face of Australia. That century and a half witnessed the slow decline of Spain, the rise and decline of the Netherlands, the rising power of England and her North American colonies. It saw a rapid increase in international commerce, the growth of science, the beginning of an industrial revolution and the birth of Watt's steam engine. It was a new Europe which the navigator James Cook left in August 1768 on the voyage which would discover the east coast of Australia. And his discovery was first made useful because of some of those changes that had severed the world of the Pilgrim Fathers from the world of James Watt.

Cook's voyage itself had been spurred by the rising interest in practical and theoretical science, for his first destination was the new-found island of Tahiti in the south Pacific, where he was to study the planet Venus as it crossed the face of the sun on 3 June 1769. To cross the world to take part in an inverted rite of sun worship does not seem to be a mission of scientific importance; but in 1769 it certainly was. By observing the transit of Venus, the distance of the sun from the earth could be computed; and that computation was fundamental to astronomy in an era when astronomy was the sister science of navigation. It was not enough to rely on observing the transit from European observatories. If the day was cloudy or unfavourable and the observation from England or France or North America was dulled, the astronomers had to wait 105 years for another chance. Hence Cook's voyage in the converted collier *Endeavour* around Cape Horn to Tahiti, which he reached seven weeks before the day of the eclipse.

Cook was then aged forty, a tall man, with long brown hair tied behind, and brown eyes arched by bushy brows. He was a cool, brave navigator, a dexterous map maker, and also a mathematician and astronomer.

The first aim of Cook's voyage had reflected England's rising interest in science and navigation, and the second aim reflected England's rising interest in new lands and new sources of trade. Between 1748 and 1775 the volume of shipping engaged in England's three long-distance routes — to North America, the West Indies, and Asia — was doubled. England understandably was more and more attracted to new lands as a source of commercial gain, and that attraction tinted the instructions given to Captain Cook. His instructions were to search the South Pacific for the mysterious south land, for at that time it was valid to speculate that the unexplored area between New Zealand and South America could not simply be ocean and nothing but ocean. The area was vast enough to conceal another Asia, and that new Asia might be as valuable for trade as the old.

At daylight on 20 April 1770, after running before a southerly gale, he saw sloping, timbered hills in the distance. For nine days he followed the coast and its blue spine of mountains, hoping that the line of surf on the beaches would suddenly give way to a safe anchorage. Eventually he found the anchorage at Botany Bay, a few miles south of where the city of Sydney now stands, and for a week Cook's men explored the shore, observed the native fishermen, gathered a pile of botanical specimens, and chattered about the strangeness of the land they had found. On the strength of differing, often vague, reports of that week in Botany Bay, the English government sixteen years later was to select it as the site for the first British settlement in the Pacific.

Cook sailed along almost the entire east coast of Australia and, though unable to tell if it was part of the same land the Dutchmen had seen to the west, he annexed it for Britain under the name of New South Wales. He completed his exploration by passing through Torres Strait to Djakarta, then home by way of Cape Town and St Helena. In England after a voyage of nearly three years he confided to a Whitby friend: 'I have made no great discoveries, yet I have explored more of the South Sea than all that have gone before me.'

Preceding pages: The *Endeavour,* Cook's command on his first great voyage to the South Seas, was the former collier *Earl of Pembroke,* built in 1764. When he was barely nineteen, Cook had worked for John Walker, a coal shipper of Whitby, and his experience with colliers in the North Sea led him to believe they would be ideally suited for exploration. (His second vessel, the *Resolution,* was also a Whitby-built collier.) The *Endeavour* was less than 30 metres long overall and her maximum beam was less than six metres. She was substantially refitted for her new purpose in which she justified Cook's assessment of her as a sturdy vessel.

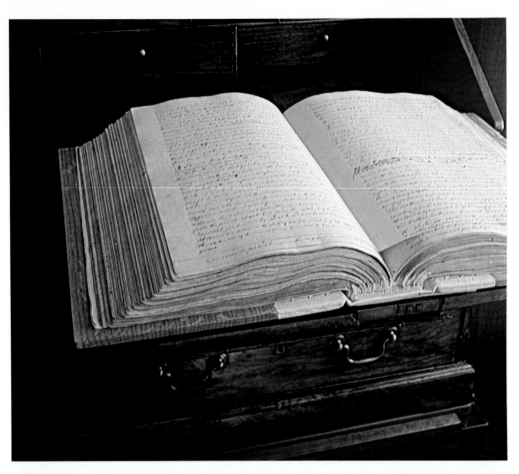

Cook was born at Marton-in-Cleveland, Yorkshire, in October 1728. As a boy he worked on Airy Holme farm, near Great Ayton, where his father was bailiff. The cottage occupied by Cook's parents at Great Ayton (right) was purchased by the philanthropist Sir Wilfrid Grimwade and brought to Melbourne to mark the city's centenary in 1932. The ivy which partly covers the cottage in Fitzroy Gardens was grown from a slip from Great Ayton. The National Library of Australia in Canberra houses even more important Cook memorabilia. Above left: The journal kept by Cook during the voyage of the *Endeavour* lies open on the navigator's writing desk. Above: Ship's compass believed to have been on board the *Endeavour.* Left: A beautifully-made 'universal sundial' thought to have been designed by Cook.

Birthplace

'... he perceived "the finest harbour in the
world, in which a thousand ships of the line
may ride in perfect security" and in it, a deep
sheltered cove.'

JOHN CURREY, *The Convict Years*

To lead the expedition to establish a penal settlement in New South Wales the Home Office chose Arthur Phillip, forty-eight years of age, a captain of the Royal Navy. Few men have been better suited to a task: Phillip was a man of rare commonsense, humanity and vision. Yet ironically these qualities seem to have played little or no part in his selection. Indeed, the man who appointed him, Lord Sydney, was to say later that little was known of the actual reason for Phillip's appointment.

The *Supply*, with Phillip's advance party, arrived in Botany Bay on 18 January 1788 only two days before the remainder of the First Fleet. It did not take long for Phillip to decide that the place was quite unsuitable for the site of a permanent settlement. The bay was too open, the soil was poor and the coastal land was surrounded by swamps. Instead he began looking at the coast to the north and, on entering Port Jackson, he perceived 'the finest harbour in the world, in which a thousand ships of the line may ride in the most perfect security' and in it, a deep sheltered cove which he named after the man who had sent him on this mission to the other side of the world, Thomas Townshend, Viscount Sydney.

The employment of the convicts was Phillip's first major problem. For he found himself with men and equipment totally unsuited to the task of establishing the settlement. Many of the convicts were too old to do any manual labour; others were too sick — scurvy and dysentery had broken out on landing — while the remainder were simply disinclined to work. 'Numbers of them,' he wrote, 'have been brought up from their infancy in such indolence that they would starve if left to themselves.' Out of roughly 730 convicts, Phillip found that, after allowing for public works, he could put only 250 to work on the land — and none of these had any sound knowledge of farming. In any case, they had brought with them nothing with which to plough the fields; instead they had to scratch away with picks and hoes and shovels which Phillip himself admitted were 'the worst that ever was seen'. Their axes bent on the hard Australian timber, the hoes snapped on the sun-baked ground. Forgetful of the southern seasons they planted their seeds at the wrong time of the year — and what little sprouted was eaten by ants and field mice. The few cattle they had brought with them from Cape Town strayed into the bush, while the sheep were attacked and eaten by dingoes. After two years at Sydney the settlement was still depending on the remainder of the stores they had brought from Cape Town and England. An exasperated Phillip found himself without even the most elementary articles of life; there was no limestone with which to make cement for buildings; shovels had to be used instead of frying pans; they had no candles; the uniforms of the marines were in tatters, and the convicts went about virtually naked.

Under these depressing conditions the convicts survived on a weekly ration from the government stores of seven pounds of bread or seven pounds of flour; seven pounds of beef or four pounds of pork; three pints of pease; six ounces of butter; one pound of flour or half a pound of rice.

Through the remainder of 1788 and the whole of 1789 conditions remained bleak. A few public stores, roads and wharfs were constructed with convict labour and there was some limited success in agriculture. But the general mood was one of discontent and disillusionment. Only Phillip held them together. He was suffering from a wound in his side caused by a native spear and he limited himself to the same ration issued to his men, but if his spirit was broken he did not show it. On the contrary, he was working out his own policy for the development of the colony. He sent a ship to Cape Town to get more supplies and with her sent messages to England asking for proper tools and utensils. He knew that the men he had would never succeed in cultivating the soil so he asked for free settlers: honest, sound men who could be attracted by large grants of land and free convict labour to work them. In this way the miserable gaol in the wilderness could be transformed.

Phillip's judgement was sound, as the Home Office was later to acknowledge, but in England the paramount desire was to clear the gaols. Lord Grenville, successor to Sydney, agreed with Phillip's comments and authorised land grants to military officers and settlers; convicts would be assigned to work the land granted and skilled men would be sent out to supervise the convict labour. But as to Phillip's vision of a new empire little was said. New South Wales was a convict settlement, and the convicts kept on coming.

On 3 June 1790, when the settlement at Sydney Cove was perilously close to starvation, the *Lady Juliana* sailed into Port Jackson bringing 221 women convicts and relief supplies. She was followed a few weeks later by the Second Fleet: the *Surprize* with 218 male convicts and part of the newly-formed colonial garrison to be known as the New South Wales Corps; the *Scarborough* and *Neptune* with another 474 men and seventy-six women convicts.

This human cargo poured ashore amid turmoil and confusion. Out of more than 1000 convicts who had sailed in this second wave almost 270 had died on the voyage and close to 500 of the survivors were ill and unable to work. In tents hastily erected around Sydney Cove the wretches now lay, consumed with fever, dysentery and scurvy.

Yet this new crisis marked the end of the beginning. For the benefits of a sunny climate soon restored the sick; full rations were resumed; tools and building supplies had arrived, and the proper work of building the settlement could begin. From that time the flow of convicts was not interrupted. In 1791 more than 2000 arrived and for the next twenty years a steady trickle of three to seven hundred was maintained.

Phillip never saw this tide of felonry matched by a flow of the free settlers he wished for. But his commitment never wavered and there were at least some other very real satisfactions. Towards the end of 1792 almost 810 hectares of rich land were under cultivation on the Parramatta River and the time was not far off when the colony would be self-supporting. Brick and tile making were under way and a few public buildings of brick and stone had been completed. In December of that year, tired and sick, he returned to England for what he hoped might be a furlough. He was not to see the colony again; he returned to naval duties, married again, rose to the rank of admiral and retired in 1805 to live on his pension at Bath. He died in 1814 and for many years was quite forgotten.

Preceding pages: Having examined, and rejected, Botany Bay as the site of a settlement, Phillip proceeded to Port Jackson. Here he wrote later: 'The different coves were examined with all possible expedition. I fixed on the one that had the best spring of water, and in which ships can anchor so close to the shore that at a very small expense quays can be made at which the largest ships may unload.' Within a few years the Sydney Cove anchorage at the mouth of the old Tank Stream would have looked similar to this reconstruction at Old Sydney Town, Gosford.

When Phillip landed at Sydney Cove in 1788 the entire population had to be housed in tents. Gradually these were replaced with huts: first for the officers and officials; later for the convicts. Most of the earliest huts had timber frames set directly into the earth with walls of saplings laid horizontally, filled with mud and whitewashed with pipeclay to help make them weather-proof. The roofs were at first formed of thatch (left) or of shingles cut from the cabbage-tree palm. The first building to be wholly constructed of bricks was the governor's cottage, completed in June 1789. By 1794 Sydney had 700 'comfortable' huts. Buildings of the early settlement have been re-created at Old Sydney Town. Below, right: The Armoury. Below: Covered wagon is an authentic replica. Right: Brig *Perseverance* at wharf.

Early Sydney's most successful farmer was the convict (seven years for breaking and entering) James Ruse. In 1789, when his sentence had expired, Phillip put him on a plot at Parramatta with the promise that if he could make himself self-sufficient he would be rewarded. Ruse proved it could be done, and in 1792 received the colony's first grant of land: 30 acres at Parramatta named Experiment Farm. The following year he sold the land to Surgeon John Harris who later built the house (below; right) which still stands. In the same year an officer, John Macarthur, built Elizabeth Farm House, also at Parramatta (lower). Macarthur was to become more wealthy than Ruse ever aspired to, but the latter had earned his own place in history. When he died in 1837 his tombstone at St John's churchyard Campbelltown recorded his claim: 'I sowd the Forst Grain'.

Lachlan Macquarie, who became Governor of New South Wales in 1810,
brought about the first major expansion of the colony since its establishment.
Macquarie was a passionate builder, and when he left the colony in 1821 his massive
public works programme had produced more than two hundred significant
buildings. His pleasure at building things was equalled only by his zeal for recording
his achievements. In Macquarie Place he commissioned the convict Francis Greenway
to erect an obelisk (right) for the ostensible purpose of measuring the roads he
had caused to be built, while to his wife he gave the distinction of being commemorated
in a greater variety of place names than any other person in Australian history.
In the Domain, Sydney, steps were built (above) to a chair carved from the sandstone
at her favourite harbour view on a road she had planned herself.

THIS OBELISK
WAS ERECTED IN
MACQUARIE PLACE
A.D. 1818.
TO RECORD THAT ALL THE
PUBLIC ROADS
LEADING TO THE INTERIOR
OF THE COLONY
ARE MEASURED FROM IT.
L. MACQUARIE ESQ
GOVERNOR

Macquarie commissioned many new churches, including the first to be built beyond Sydney and Parramatta. His favourite architect was Francis Greenway, a short, red-haired, egocentric man with a bad temper, who had been transported for forging a contract. Pardoned by Macquarie in 1817, he became the Governor's civil architect and designed some delightful buildings in the Georgian style including Macquarie Lighthouse, St James' Church, Hyde Park and St Matthew's, Windsor (above, right). This church, built between 1817 and 1820, exemplified Greenway's talents.

The slightly austere Georgian grandeur of Macquarie's public buildings set a standard for future private and public construction. Far right: Government House Parramatta was built in 1815–16. Right: The 'doctors' house' at Windsor, named because doctors occupied it for more than a century. Below: the 'rum hospital' in Sydney was opened in 1816. It was built for the government by a group of contractors in return for exclusive rights to import 270 000 litres of rum; part of it became the New South Wales Parliament House in 1829. Below, right: Colonnade of Victoria Barracks, Paddington (1848), 225 metres long.

'Sydney sandstone' became a popular building material of colonial times. At first the stone was extracted by random quarrying of the outcrops around the township, especially from the West Rocks. Later, Macquarie established a government quarry on the north-west of Fort Phillip (Observatory) Hill. Because of the labour and expense involved in quarrying, sandstone was at first used extensively only in government buildings. An early example was the cottage (below) built in 1816 for John Cadman, Superintendent of Government Boats, near The Rocks. Other Georgian sandstone buildings resemble the house at Balmain (far right); 'Bell-Vue House', Berrima (right); cottage at Hunters Hill (below, right).

A major purpose of Cook's voyage on the *Endeavour* had been to observe the transit of Venus across the face of the sun from an ideal vantage point in the South Seas. Eighty years later the problems of survival were so far behind the citizens of Sydney that they, too, could embark on a serious study of the heavens. Lieutenant Dawes had set up a temporary observatory on The Rocks in 1788 and Sir Thomas Brisbane had helped establish a small private observatory near Government House at Parramatta in 1821 but by 1847 observation from Parramatta had ceased. The navigator Phillip Parker King saw to it that the instruments were kept, however, and in 1851 recommended a new observatory with a revolving dome. In 1858 the stone building was opened on Observatory Hill near the spot where once windmills had ground the settlement's first grain.

The Rocks area was Sydney's early commercial and maritime quarter, packed with warehouses, pubs, flophouses and seamen from around the world. Named for its rocky outcrops of sandstone, it was the site of some of the tents of Phillip's party, of the first hospital, the first windmills and the first gaol (executions took place on Gallows Hill behind the gaol). Later as a wharf precinct it boasted such establishments as The Whaler's Arms, The Hero of Waterloo (still trading) and Labor in Vain whose sign was a woman scrubbing a negro. For many years it was Sydney's most unsavoury quarter. Above: Argyle Bond Store buildings (1830). Right: Well-preserved terraces of the 1840s in Argyle Place.

Convicts

'In that furnace of gaol and whorehouse they laboured to secure a foundation upon which British civilization might awkwardly erect itself.'

JOHN RITCHIE, *Australia As Once We Were*

From 1787 to 1868 the British government transported nearly 162 000 convicts to the Australian penal settlements. Most of them landed in New South Wales and Van Diemen's Land in the 1820s and 1830s. The courts had sentenced half of them for seven years and a quarter for life. About 75 per cent of the prisoners were single, nearly all belonged to the labouring classs and most came from urban areas. The bulk of them were persistent if not habitual criminals who preyed on their fellow-men. Probably two-thirds of them had recorded former convictions. Eight out of every ten were transported for some kind of theft. One in six were women and 20 per cent of these 'on the town'. Of all the convicts two-thirds were English, about one-third Irish, and less than five per cent Scots; two-thirds claimed to subscribe to the Protestant faiths, one-third to Catholicism. In the early period as many as half their number were illiterate. Their average age was twenty-six years. In general youth was their only asset.

As a group the convicts were not gallant poachers or village Hampdens, 'more sinned against than sinning', but human flotsam thrown up by the dislocation as the Industrial Revolution pounded England out of the eighteenth and into the nineteenth century. They were also the products of Ireland's pitiful rituals of economic despair.

When finally lagged most criminals faced charges of offences against property: larceny or house-breaking, picking pockets or shop-lifting. A small minority had committed offences against the person: charged with stealing two half-crowns, one man declared 'they were won from a man with thimbles. He wanted them back and I assaulted him.' Another confessed 'I cut my wife's throat because she cohabited with other men.' Ann Ruffey stated that 'a man called Crawley took some liberties; I was tipsy and stabbed him in the side.' And Elizabeth Cleveland 'threw vitriol over George Day. I did this in a passion. He struck me first.'

Although the voyage to Australia suffered from severe restrictions, considerable operating difficulties and problematical profits, the conclusion of the Napoleonic Wars created a surplus of tonnage and intense competition on all trade routes. Some firms, whose vessels had lugged slaves to America and soldiers to Europe, competed to carry convicts to New South Wales and, in time, to convey free migrants. It took the transports 821 voyages to bring the convicts from Britain to Australia. As ships got faster and larger the average length of the trip dropped from 258 days in 1787–88 to 89 days in 1867–68, the average number of convicts each ship carried rose from 126 to 280. Beneath the hatches and the gratings, crammed in poorly ventilated holds which reeked of excrement and bilge-water, the felons suffered many privations.

On their arrival in Sydney or Hobart Town an official questioned the convicts about their conduct and treatment during the voyage, entered their physical appearance and their crimes and their sentences in a vast book of reckoning, and then directed them to government employment or distributed them as servants among the settlers. In that furnace of gaol and whorehouse they laboured to secure a foundation upon which British civilization might awkwardly erect itself. Until the early 1820s the government retained the services of many male convicts with experience in farming and in the building trades, much to the chagrin of individual landholders; it also retained the aged and the crippled, for no one else would take them. The government housed its workers in barracks, drab Bastilles in whose dormitories seventy men slept in hammocks slung twenty inches apart. At irregular intervals Authority checked that the labourers had washed their bodies, and employed barbers to shave their jaws and clip their hair. It provided their slops — a yellow or grey jacket and a waistcoat of coarse cloth, a pair of duck trousers, two cotton shirts, worsted stockings, a neckerchief, a woollen cap and, when possible, shoes; in summer the allowance extended to a smock frock and a straw hat. It also provided their food — generally one pound of flour and one pound of meat per man per day, the meat being corned beef or mutton, salt beef or pork, together with a ration (not exceeding in cost one-halfpenny per man per day) of potatoes or pumpkin. Thus fortified the convicts went forth to labour in the service of their lords.

The unskilled cleared the land, worked on the roads, dug coal or gathered grass for forage. Their brothers, the smiths and the carpenters, the bricklayers and the stonemasons, built courthouse and church, lighthouse and villa, attempting at one stage to bring Regency Bath to parts of New South Wales. They began work at 5 a.m. in summer and at 8 a.m. in winter, rested an hour over midday dinner, and laid down their tools at sunset. Barrack lights went out at 8 p.m. At times the convicts could work Saturday afternoons on their own behalf, earning money for such luxuries as tea and tobacco. On Sunday they dressed in their best and were marched to divine service where some clergyman, offended by their stink, told them that the Lord was their shepherd, therefore they could lack nothing. His listeners remained unconvinced.

Labour was a lottery. Independent of their period of sentence, the mechanics and farmers worked longest, while the weak and the sickly, the unskilled and the plain lazy, moved oceans in fathoming means of evasion. The chains of Newgate had been unshackled, but in their stead felons were bound to hew wood and draw water and feed the blistering brick-kiln. And ever under the supervisory eye of some officious army underling, quick-tempered and all-scarlet, or some convict overseer, one of their own kind, who stooped and truckled to ingratiate himself with his masters while being detested by them, by his comrades, and by himself.

The sense of grievance and the despair of the gaoled was measured against the callousness and the sense of guilt of the gaolers; whining submissiveness or sullen resentment was met by arrogance, or vindictiveness, or plain cruelty. A social division separated rogue and respectable, but the respectable were brutalized by their colonial experience. A convict arriving late for work might have his rations reduced or be made to labour on Saturday afternoon; absence from work, or insolence, or theft, were punished by solitary confinement, or by a term in the Gaol Gang, or by flogging. Punishment, too, bore all the features of a lottery: its effect varied according to the bodily and mental strength of the recipient. The fifty year-old Thomas Williams' mind and body snapped while serving twelve months on bread and water; another, Michael Hoare,

Preceding pages: Throughout the years of transportation to the Australian colonies the convict's irons were a universal symbol of servitude. Leg irons effectively hobbled convicts in government labour gangs, making escape difficult; manacles (pictured) were sometimes prescribed in addition and, in extreme cases, other more sadistic devices. Irons were secured by a metal rivet inserted and fastened by a blacksmith whose services, under normal circumstances, were also required to strike off the pin when the convict was to be set free. Leg irons weighed about seventeen kilograms and were joined by a chain kept off the ground by a string looped through the convict's belt.

feigned insanity to gain release. The lash degraded both the flogger and the flogged. A cat of whipped twine was used on lesser offenders, one of knotted twine on thieves and those of 'mutinous disposition'. The Very Reverend William Ullathorne, the Catholic Vicar General, knew one felon who in three years had received 1600 lashes. Magistrates could order punishments of up to 200 strokes, though in practice floggings rarely exceeded 100, the most usual being 25 or 50 — nowhere near the number inflicted in the services, if that were any solace to the victim. The wallopings in the Barrack began at 12.30 p.m., the sessions lasting between thirty minutes and two hours. Men were lashed on the back, boys on the breech. In the hope of driving home a salutary lesson the authorities assembled prisoners to witness the thrashings, just as they herded them together to see the gallows do her work.

The recalcitrant were sent to secondary penal stations which provided horrors beyond the comprehension of their Downing Street architects. At Newcastle some lime quarrymen were blinded; most suffered agonies when carrying sacks of the stuff through the waves to waiting ships, for the lime once wet ran into the floggers' wounds upon their backs and stung unmercifully. At Moreton Bay careless or tired lags were crushed beneath the trees they felled or lost their toes from clumsy axework. At Port Arthur human beasts of burden were made to push railway coaches. At Norfolk Island the inhumanity of the commandant, Captain John Price, made convicts weep with gratitude when they heard that the death sentence had been passed upon them.

Some convicts, more brave or desperate than the rest, thought that death was not the only escape. Between 1803 and 1820, 265 of them attempted to flee from captivity. The number who gained liberty will probably never be known. It was relatively easy to scale the barrack wall by night, easier still to bolt from the ranks of a government road gang as it shuffled to its place of labour or to run away from an ill-guarded hospital. The bush provided conceal-ment and freedom tasted sweet.

The majority of felons realized that the safest way out of their gaolers' cage lay in the passage of time and the expiration of their sentences. As an incentive to reformation and good conduct successive governors dangled before them the prospect of even earlier freedom. If well-behaved, a convict could receive a ticket-of-leave (which permitted him to work for himself within an assigned district, providing he reported regularly to the authorities), or a conditional pardon (which set him at liberty so long as he did not leave the colony), or an absolute pardon (which granted him total emancipation). In 1813 Governor Lachlan Macquarie, whose experiences among the disinherited in Mull and Bombay had helped shape his humanitarianism, drew up a set of regulations affecting the eligibility of convicts for these indulgences. In practice Macquarie chose to err on the side of leniency, allowing almost 500 exceptions to his stipulations. While there was liberality, there was also randomness. Many of the prisoners who had built the road across the mountains to Bathurst, and some of their wealthy fellows who had merely lent horses and carts for the undertaking, obtained pardons; meantime poorer but better conducted convicts remained ignored.

Macquarie and his predecessors — Phillip, Hunter, King and Bligh — also used small land grants as rewards for emancipated convicts, as incentives to their continued reformation, and as a means of establishing an economy self-sufficient in foodstuffs. These governors envisaged a prosperous yeomanry. Some ex-convicts fulfilled their liege-lord's vision, as did George Best who had formerly farmed in Sussex, and in their cups toasted their patron as 'prince of men'. But most were disillusioned and dashed by the agricultural experiment. In 1821 Patrick Hart estimated that only one in eight emancipists had made a success of farming and considered that this proportion would decline as land granted further from the city markets increased cartage costs.

Macquarie raised a handful of his favourite emancipists to positions of authority and endeavoured to introduce them to the society of government house. Four of them he made magistrates, two he permitted to practise as attorneys, one became principal superintendent of convicts, another colonial civil architect, a third an antipodean poet laureate. One emancipist leader, Edward Eagar, considered that the moral conduct of the ex-convicts — whether rich or poor — was as good as that in any British colony and a damned deal better than in many English manufacturing districts. Person and Property were safe in Australia: if that were not proof of real practical reformation, then Eagar confessed he was at a loss to know what could be. But the men in Downing Street preferred to accept the views and standards of Sir Edward Parry, the Australian Agricultural Company's commissioner between 1829–34, who felt that only three of the 800 convicts he knew had chosen the path of virtue. They chose to listen to their Reverences Robert Cartwright and William Cowper, Samuel Marsden and Thomas Scott, William Broughton and William Ullathorne. These vicars of Christ found weighty evidence of sin and depravity among the emancipists in the penal settlements: they thieved, they gamed, they got drunk, they profaned the Sabbath, they blasphemed. Indeed, there was one named Tambourine Sal who could not speak without swearing.

And so it was that witnesses testified before William Molesworth and his Committee of Inquiry in 1837. The members of Molesworth's Committee found the people of New South Wales wallowing in a sensual sty; that was bad enough. But, even worse, the colonials were liking it; and, worst of all, they saw nothing wrong with it. Molesworth reported to the House of Commons in 1838. Members of parliament decided that transportation to New South Wales should cease in 1840. Molesworth and his learned colleagues feared that the canker of convictdom would spread, corrupting the free inhabitants of Australia in their thoughts and in their deeds.

It was left to a young man who visited Sydney Town in 1836 to pass fair and final judgement. That man looked into the heart of the matter and did not draw back afraid. He was to write on the very origin and nature of life. His name was Charles Darwin. Of the convict system in New South Wales he reported:

'On the whole, as a place of punishment, the object is scarcely gained; as a real system of reform it has failed, as perhaps would every other plan; but as a means of making men outwardly honest, — of converting vagabonds, most useless in one hemisphere, into active citizens of another, and thus giving birth to a new and splendid country — a grand centre of civilization — it has succeeded to a degree perhaps unparalleled in history.'

For Darwin saw that an unclean thing could be made clean; that transportation, despite its failings, had wrought great changes within its dross. He also saw that the lotus fed on dung; that convictdom had prepared a new world for those who would follow — for the free and the native-born, for the Inheritors.

Convicts stationed in central Sydney were housed in the Hyde Park barracks at the top of Macquarie Street. During the day they laboured in gangs at public works such as roads and bridge-building, harbour works, quarrying, making bricks or constructing the Governor's residence at Darlinghurst Gaol (right). In the outer settlements well-behaved convicts were 'assigned' to free settlers as a source of cheap labour, sometimes under conditions not far above slavery. Below: Clock surmounting facade of Hyde Park Barracks completed in 1817 and designed by Francis Greenway. Below, left: Gate in wall to barracks building. Below, right: Convict-made brick with the word 'Berrima' roughly incised.

Norfolk Island, off the east coast of New South Wales, was settled shortly after the arrival of the First Fleet and served as a sub-colony and penal settlement until 1814. During this period and again in later years, it was notorious as an island prison under a series of commandants whose demeanour ranged from the enlightenment of Alexander Maconachie to the sadism of the hated and feared John Price. In 1824 the British Government ruled that the island was to become a place of banishment for the 'worst type' of convicts and Governor Ralph Darling was to write three years later that: 'My object was to hold out that Settlement as a place of the extremest punishment, short of Death'.

Port Arthur (below) on the south-east coast of Tasmania was the site of the largest penal station of colonial Australia. Thought to be escape-proof because it could be reached only by crossing the isthmus of Eaglehawk Neck, it was the grim home for thousands of convicts between 1830 and 1877. The inmates of Port Arthur were mostly put to various labouring tasks during the day. There was a non-denominational church (right) and attendance at chapel was compulsory, but critics of the penal system saw not the slightest sign that this produced reform.
Far right: Sandstone lion by Richard Paterson outside officers' quarters.

Over page: Ruins of the four-storey penitentiary (centre, with chimney). Built in 1848, the brick structure could house 657 convicts in cells and dormitories. The better-behaved convicts were kept on the top floor in the dormitories. The remainder slung their hammocks in cells measuring 2.4 by 1.5 metres on the first and second floors. The mess-room where the convicts had their meals was on the third floor. Battlements of the guardhouse and magazine are in the foreground.

The castle-like Round Tower (right; above; left) surmounted Port Arthur's guardhouse and magazine, a stone structure built in 1835. Left: Interior of the Model Prison. Here the scourge of the lash was replaced with the tyranny of the 'Silent System'. In the belief that physical punishment merely brutalised hardened lags, penal reformers prescribed an environment of total silence in which the incorrigible could reflect and repent without distraction.

Over page: Those who died in servitude were buried on the Island of the Dead in Port Arthur Bay. Of 1646 recorded graves only 180, those of prison staff and military personnel, are marked.

Convict architects, masons and labourers employed their talents on public works. The cost of their upkeep was negligible and their craftsmanship was often of a very high standard. The three-span Macquarie Bridge (above; right) at Ross in the Tasmanian Midlands was built from local sandstone in 1836 by John Lee Archer, using convict labour. Richmond Bridge (top) over the Coal River was built in 1823 to the design of the Tasmanian Colonial Architect David Lambe and is the oldest standing bridge in Australia.

The years which followed the cessation of transportation saw the relics of both felonry and free settlers merge imperceptibly into the landscape. Far left: Joseph Moir's 60 metre tower, near Taroona, Tasmania, was built in 1870 to make shot. It affords a commanding view of the Derwent River estuary. Below: Observatory at Wickham Terrace, Brisbane, was built by convict labour in 1829. It was first used as a windmill. Left: Shop and cottages at Richmond, Tasmania, a former military post and convict station. Below, left: Historic stone church (1848) at Buckland, Tasmania.

The transportation of convicts to New South Wales was abolished in 1840. But in Western Australia settlement by free men was proving arduous and in 1849 Fremantle settlers demanded a large-scale penal settlement to provide labour. The British Government was happy to oblige and the first shipload of convicts arrived in 1850. The transportees at first carried out public works at Fremantle and Perth; later a number of country depots were established in the hope of assisting agricultural development. Far left: Ruins of Lynton convict depot. Left; below, right: Convict commandant's residence. Below, left: Convict graves, Lynton.

Settlers

'The sense of expansion that came with the squatting years attracted men who saw in the new country the fulfilment of their dreams.'

R M YOUNGER, *The Pioneer Years*

From the early 1820s the colonial grasslands offered boundless opportunity for those of the middle classes whose ambitions outran their scope for advancement in Britain. Newspapers and magazines in London and Edinburgh began to speculate on the potential of an apparently limitless territory in New South Wales where land grants could be obtained freely. In a setting where social standing and economic success had traditionally gone with great landholdings, there seemed every reason for the shrewd and adventurous to assemble all available resources and set off on the great adventure. The little settlement of Sydney, for so long no more than a tiny window looking in on a vast unknown continent, became the main channel for pastoral expansion.

By this time English millowners were prepared to buy as much fine wool as could be supplied to them; and the experience of practical men in New South Wales and Van Diemen's Land had already shown that wool of excellent quality could be produced on the colony's pastures. The land might be equally good for cattle, but sheep, giving an annual yield of a non-perishable and keenly-sought commodity, became the major reason for opening up the land.

Under the sheepmen's pressure, expansion of inland settlement was accelerating in spite of official attempts to hold it in check. In 1829 Governor Darling defined the 'limits of occupation' as being the Nineteen Counties — a total area of about 90 000 square kilometres — but the pastures of the out-of-bounds hinterland by now held an irresistible appeal for ambitious stockowners. The situation was ambiguous; on the one hand the Government was encouraging the sale and occupation of the land it nominated, while beyond an invisible boundary it was attempting to forbid occupation of tracts which seemed equally good, if not better. For more than thirty years tickets of occupation conferring the right to pasture flocks on Crown land had been issued; now neither these nor the system of licences, introduced in 1826, could keep up with the infiltration.

Sheepmen were moving far and wide on the western side of the ranges. Those who moved out and took up holdings were known as 'squatters' — derisively at first, but later officially — as they entered on land to which they had no title. The squatters' occupation proceeded in leapfrog fashion, with newcomers moving farther out. If the land promised well, the new squatter decided how much he wanted for his run. The thought of 'helping themselves' to the grass appealed as much to the stockowners as it did to their sheep and cattle.

The dweller beyond the frontier found himself in complete isolation. As he and his few companions moved deeper into the bush, they left behind the trappings of the civilised world, and faced the problems of existence in an untamed and empty land. The fear of isolation had to be overcome, and although some cast off all anxiety, many remained haunted by the loneliness.

Nevertheless, the sense of expansion that came with the squatting years attracted men who saw in the new country the fulfilment of their dream. Most of those who launched themselves as squatters were men of reasonable capital, perhaps £2000 or £3000; however, if a man was willing to do much of the work himself he might begin with £400 or £500, and there were even cases of working men and ex-convicts who had been given a few sheep and cattle as recompense by graziers, and who were able to start with virtually no money at all. For a basic ten pounds a year licence fee and a penny a head for all stock grazed, a squatter could take up whatever land he could lay claim to. To look after each

500 sheep he employed a shepherd to whom he paid £52 a year. Shearing cost one pound for each 100 sheep. With an average fleece weighing about 1.1 kilogram, the sheepowner might expect to receive anything from three to four shillings a head for the wool, according to the state of the English market.

In some ways what was happening in the Australian bush was similar to the experience of settlers who had faced the North American wilderness two centuries earlier. Just as those earlier English settlers, as they pushed out from the footholds along the Atlantic shore, had found their lives moulded by the conditions of the new world, so those who moved into the Australian inland had to develop inner resources to cope with the solitude of the big land they had entered.

Matched only by the appetite of the sheep for grass was the flockowners' zeal for land. Governor Gipps wrote in 1840: 'As well might it be attempted to confine the Arabs of the Desert within a circle drawn on the sands as to confine the graziers or woolgrowers of New South Wales within any bounds that can possibly be assigned to them; and as certainly as the Arabs would be starved so also would the flocks and herds of New South Wales, if they were so confined, and the prosperity of the country would be at an end.' The grazier, if he was lucky, might finish up occupying tens of thousands of acres. Established landowners became part-squatters, pasturing some of their flocks on their home stations and some beyond the official boundaries under the management of their sons or overseers.

The new squatters might buy a flock and acquire the occupied run with it, but most of the squatters in the early phase were men who took their sheep and a few cattle, with drays and provisions, to the outskirts of the occupied area, where they pre-empted whatever land they could prudently occupy. The first task was to cut timber and make a rough yard. Sometimes it was necessary to clear a little land. Then a few days were required to build a simple hut from the materials at hand. In some districts the nature of the timber made this a simple task: wide strips of bark could be stretched on a framework of heavy saplings. In other cases a more elaborate dwelling might be built with large upright slabs of timber, fitted top and bottom into heavy sleepers. In such a hut the squatter and his men might camp for months on end, living on salt meat and damper, and tea without milk.

After the squatter took up his main holding, he might go on and set up an 'outstation' or two. Once the site was decided on, by forward scouting, the operation was simple. 'Having discovered an abundant supply of feed and water,' one successful squatter recalled, 'a day sufficed to bring my sheep to the spot, and the scanty requirements of an out-station of the sort were quickly supplied. Merrily with saw and axe we felled the trees around, and with them constructed the required yards, a tarpaulin and a few forked sticks and poles

Preceding pages: Early in 1835 George Evans, a building contractor and sheep owner, was talking to his friend John Pascoe Fawkner in the Cornwall Hotel, Launceston. There, a fellow-Tasmanian, John Batman, told them of the immense tracts of land he had recently acquired on Port Phillip Bay. Evans and Fawkner decided to make their own investigation; they sailed in August on the *Enterprise*, and by the following year Evans had found the ideal run for his flock: low-lying land in the valley near Sunbury where emus roamed. There he built his pleasant white-washed sandstone homestead 'Emu Bottom' which still stands, carefully restored, the oldest homestead in Victoria.

being all that was necessary in the way of a hut for the shepherds. Then, having stripped for the men a sheet of bark each, on which to lay their beds, I left them almost as pleased with the change as the sheep themselves, and I returned with my overseer to the head station.'

The wise landseeker had an eye for selecting not only a good tract of sheep pasture but a favourable homestead site within it. Shrewder men usually chose rising ground offering views over the run, where the homestead could be defended if necessary, and close to permanent water. To avoid being entirely cut off from whatever passing traffic there might be, some preferred a spot not too far from teamsters' existing tracks, or one close to the line they believed others might eventually follow on their way to points farther out. A slab or bark hut was usually the initial dwelling, but occasionally the settler with a family built a simple weatherboard homestead from the start. Such buildings were rather more substantial but still quite elemental in design. Sometimes they had a room on each side of a hallway which ran from the kitchen to the front door; and sometimes they were not more than a square divided in two, without a hallway. A general concession to the Australian climate was the addition of a lean-to verandah, low and often quite wide, to provide shade on the facade and some protection to the front door.

The squatter usually went through two phases in establishing himself: the initial or struggling stage, when he had plenty to do and profits were certain to be meagre because of the commitments he had to meet; and the second, when — provided his early endeavours had been successful — he could enjoy life a little more, even if it were still in a slab hut. Edward M. Curr, an extremely successful squatter on the Murray and the son of the Van Diemen's Land Company manager, recorded his adventures as a young man in the early 1840s. By this time he had won the race for land and established his estate, and leisure time had become abundant for him.

'At that period reading became our chief resource,' he wrote. 'In the matter of books I believe we were better off than most of our neighbours, though those in our possession had been got together in a haphazard sort of way, at various times and without any idea of making a collection for the bush. However, from a pair of wooden pegs in the wall-plate of the sitting room of our rough, but not uncomfortable, slab hut at Tongala, surrounded by a miscellaneous collection of fire-arms, foils, masks, wooden sabres, fencing gloves, stockwhips, spurs, and other articles which embellished the walls, hung, in the place of honour, some shelves made of bark, on which were ranged our literary treasures. These volumes, our great resource for years against ennui, for want of something new, were read, re-read, and discussed I cannot say how often . . .'

The eagerness of men such as this in establishing their sheep-runs played a great part in the wool saga that stretched half-way round the world to involve England's woolspinners and the stockbreeders of Europe as well as the colonies. By 1840 Australia had supplanted Germany as England's chief supplier of fine wool. In northern German provinces the principle of selection as a means of improving the quality of merino fleeces had long been recognised by sheepbreeders as important, and men followed it as a trade. Some of these men, and other British stockbreeders, were brought to Australia to help in the improvement of flocks.

With all these aids to success, the grazier still ran the risk of big losses and even financial failure. It was a rule of the wise and cautious to put all their available funds — but no more — into sheep and other livestock, and to keep other outlays to a minimum. Other men involved themselves in debt, or built up big commitments, and failed to survive the slumps and droughts. When that happened, sudden changes of fortune took place. Even neighbours found that their adjoining land varied enormously in carrying capacity, so that one might prosper and the other fail. Confounding the cautious and the gambler alike was the unpredictableness of seasonal conditions from year to year. The droughts of the late 1830s came when wool prices were high; then wool prices fell back sharply when better seasons returned.

In 1842, just when the rapid build-up of flocks resulted in wool shipments exceeding the demand, the London market was hit by depression. The wool price collapsed, and to add to the stockowners' problems, a severe drought spread over an extensive area. From being ready buyers of stock, men were suddenly desperate sellers; but the capital inflow had dried up and in 1843 three banks failed. Country properties in which thousands of pounds had been invested were sold for a few hundred; sheep brought a shilling or less a head. There were hundreds of insolvencies. It took two years for wool prices to return to profitable levels, and by that time a new crop of optimists had moved into the pastoral industry. Recovery and expansion went hand in hand. The land south of the Murray produced 1800 tonnes of wool, worth £174 000 in 1844; the following year, when the wool market had recovered, the clip rose to nearly 3200 tonnes and earnings reached almost £400 000. The rich pastures of the Port Phillip district were outstripping the rest of New South Wales in the volume of wool produced, and the fleeces grown there were averaging higher prices than most others.

Perhaps the most remarkable feature of the squatters' initial takeover of the land was the orderliness and speed with which it was accomplished. In the continent's south-eastern crescent a great province of grass as big as France was occupied in a very short time by men who found land to their liking and then, by persuasion, managed to hold off other landseekers following on their heels.

The early settlers quickly learned to utilise the materials of the bush. Wide overlapping sheets of ironbark or stringybark were lashed to a sapling frame with greenhide to make a weatherproof roof. The hut on the East Ballarat goldfields (far left) had a chimney and low 'walls' of mud-bricks. Later, more substantial structures were built of wattle-and-daub: thin branches, usually of acacia (wattle), were woven basket-fashion between the frame. Mud was then forced into the wattling and the surface smoothed down. Left: hut at Tambaroora, New South Wales. Below, left: Fauchery's hut replica Sovereign Hill, Victoria. Below: Hut from Tanjil goldfields, Gippsland Folk Museum, Victoria.

The slab hut was another bushman's innovation. The shepherd's hut (right; below, right) originally stood at Raglan, Victoria, in the 1840s. It has sturdy walls of timber slabs fitted into the frame, bark roof and well-fitted stone hearth. The floor is of mud mixed with fresh cow-manure and the beds have 'bush-feather' mattresses: wool bags and flour sacks stuffed with gum leaves.
Far right: The hut at 'Glenmore' homestead, Rockhampton, Queensland, was built in 1858 with a mixture of log and slab construction. Below: a simple wooden cradle c. 1850 from the Earlystreet Village, Brisbane. Made from Queensland hoop pine, it could be rocked by the mother's foot.

At George Evans' 'Emu Bottom' homestead the kitchen fire burned continuously through summer and winter, for there was no stove. Pots and pans were hung from hooks or chains or from the cooking crane. Meat could be cooked either on a spit or in a camp oven which was placed among the coals and could be used also for cakes or scones. Once or twice a week bread was made in the bread oven. Food was kept in zinc-wired safes and bulk supplies in a special place in the roof. Washing was done in wooden buckets and the kitchen duties also included making candles and soap, butter and cheese. Right: The blacksmith's shop. Below, left: Split timber shingles of verandah roof. Below, right: Old chain embedded in eucalypt.

By 1839 the settlement of the Port Phillip District (later to become the State of Victoria) was proceeding so rapidly that the colonial administration in New South Wales decided that a resident official was needed, with the powers of a lieutenant-governor. When Charles Joseph La Trobe arrived in October of that year to take up his post as Superintendent of the Port Phillip District he brought with him the components of a prefabricated house. It was a simple weatherboard cottage with shutters on the windows and a wooden shingle roof. It was originally erected in present-day East Melbourne but was later restored and re-located on the Melbourne Domain. The timber-panelled bedroom (over page) is furnished with articles of the period.

Settlers in the infant townships of the 1850s lived simply enough but the comforts they enjoyed presented a stark contrast to the hardships of life in the bush. In 1854 Charles Pain was sent to take charge of the Post Office at Ballarat. The building was new and so was the residence provided for the Post Master. The well-fitted kitchen (far left; above) and the piano in the living room were unmistakable signs that Pain and his family were relatively well-to-do. Pain's Post Office and residence, which once stood at the corner of Lydiard and Mair streets, have been re-built, from the original plans, at Sovereign Hill Historical Park.

Public houses followed the settlers in town and country. The 'Hero of Waterloo' cellars, Sydney (below, right) date back to the 1840s. Further afield, hotels served as staging posts and resting places for travellers over the continent's vast distances. Far right: Rhoden's Halfway House stood on a busy Cobb & Co. route east of Pakenham, Victoria. It has been restored at the Gippsland Folk Museum. Right: The Red Feather Inn (c. 1846) at Hadspen, Tasmania. Below: Historic inn at Berrima, New South Wales.

While settlers in south-eastern Australia were still clearing the bush, the pioneers of Tasmania were comfortably settled. 'Entally' (right) with its stables (far right) was built by Thomas Reiby on the banks of the South Esk in the 1820s. The stables (above) at 'Brickendon', near Longford, were built between 1828 and 1830.

Western Australia was settled at Albany on King George Sound in 1826; 'Strawberry Hill' farm (left; right) was the home of the government resident. The two-storey section was constructed in 1836 for Sir Richard Spencer who brought with him from England the doors, flooring, windows and roofing slate. The farm is the oldest dwelling-place in the west. Below: Old dray at New Norfolk, Tasmania. Below, right: Outbuildings of 'Highfield' at Stanley, Tasmania, one-time headquarters of the Van Diemen's Land Company pastoral syndicate.

Tasmania's New Norfolk district was settled early in the nineteenth century by families from Norfolk Island. Here, in the 1820s, one of the settlers, William Abel, built the King's Head Inn comprising, initially, 'a large brick dwelling, stable, barn and three outhouses'. Abel lost the property in a foreclosure and in the 1850s the then owners took up hop-farming and re-named the property 'Valleyfield'. Right; below, left: Stone outhouses. Below: Doors of the coach house.

Over page: 'Glenrock', at Marulan, New South Wales, was built in the early 1840s by grazier George Barber. His first house was mud-plastered and measured 12.2 metres by 7.9 metres but his family increased as fast as his fortunes and he later built the classic Georgian homestead whose fluted columns were each carved from a single piece of sandstone.

From his relatively modest start at
Elizabeth Farm, Parramatta, John
Macarthur had become, by the 1830s one of
the leading pastoralists in the colonies; a
wealthy man and a pioneer sheep-breeder.
Through the influence of Lord Camden,
Macarthur received land grants totalling
4000 hectares which could be sited wherever
he thought the prospects for wool-growing
would be most suitable. Macarthur chose to
take up his land in the rich Cowpastures
area south-west of Sydney. He named his
new property 'Camden Park' and
determined to set the seal on his life's work
and career by commissioning the architect
John Verge to design a great mansion
(above). He was well into his sixties when
Verge drew up the plans in 1831 and he
died before the house was completed,
leaving his sons James and William to
become its first real owners. Right: The
library, 'Camden'.

Captain John Coghill, a Scots mariner and trader, gave up the sea in 1826 and settled on the land in New South Wales. A wealthy man, he was not obliged to face the spartan life of the bush hut which was the lot of so many other settlers, and his home 'Bedervale' at Braidwood may even have been designed by 'Camden's' architect John Verge. In any case, it was an impressive pile, 21.35 metres long; and great quantities of cedar and french polish went into its building, which took several years to complete. Above: Main entrance. Left: The drawing room.

The limestone 'Canberry Plains' which
straddled the Molonglo River in New
South Wales were first crossed by
Charles Throsby in 1820. Some of the
early settlers' buildings, like Blundell's
farmhouse (far right), still stand. In the
following decades the pioneer holdings
were dwarfed by sheep stations like
Murray's 'Yarralumla' which ran to
than 16 000 hectares. Lanyon station
(right; below right) was begun in 1835.
St John's church, Canberra, (below)
with its whitewashed schoolhouse, was
completed in 1845. A tombstone of that
year in its churchyard bears the
prescient inscription: 'For here we have
no continuing city, but seek one
to come.'

96

Goldrush

'. . . he showed them likely places to dig and how to wash for gold. Soon the 48 kilometres of track to Ophir were marked with the hooves of horses . . .'
GEOFFREY BLAINEY, *The Rush That Never Ended*

Before long, alluvial deposits were worked out; shafts had to be sunk and tunnels excavated along seams of gold-bearing ore. Below, left: From the vantage point of his tent the gold commissioner surveyed a moonscape of mullock-heaps and shafts. Left; below: The shaft was topped by a sapling frame supporting the windlass and shored-up with timbers to prevent cave-ins. Right: As the shaft became deeper, the claim sprouted its canvas windsail which could be turned into the prevailing breeze to funnel clean air into the shaft and tunnels below.

Diggers were compelled to buy a government licence to mine for gold. Both the licence fees and the methods of policing the system incensed the miners, and a mass meeting of miners on Bakery Hill, Ballarat, on 29 November 1854 voted to burn their licences. Next day police made a licence check and feelings ran high. The diggers formed an assembly at which, under a newly-made blue flag bearing the stars of the Southern Cross, 500 took an oath to 'fight to defend our rights and liberties'. They elected Peter Lalor 'commander-in-chief' and and proceeded to a hastily-built barricade on the site of the Eureka mining claim to prepare for a fight. It came a few days later, on 3 December, when 152 soldiers and 100 police stormed the 'stockade'. At least 30 miners and six police died and many were wounded. The miners' tents were torn down and burned; the Southern Cross was bayoneted and tied to the tail of a trooper's horse. Lalor, wounded, went into hiding. The police won but the 'Eureka Stockade' caused consternation throughout the colonies and the following year the licence system was abolished. Below: 1842 musket used by a soldier of the 12th regiment at Eureka.

In the footsteps of the diggers came the shopkeepers. Many remained on the fields and prospered long after the inexperienced 'new-chums' had returned to the cities with their pockets empty. The early canvas towns which sprouted overnight on the diggings gave way to more substantial settlements. The main street of Sovereign Hill Historical Park is an authentic reconstruction of many of the buildings which stood in central Ballarat in the 1850s. They include Thomas Bath's stables, which also housed the Cobb & Co. office; the *Ballarat Times* office; Clarke Brothers' grocery; John Reid's New York Bakery; the United States Hotel and Victoria Theatre where bawdy goldfields entertainments were held; the Colonial Bank of Australasia; John Alloo's Chinese restaurant and Robinson and Wayne's Apothecaries' Hall.

Fortunate and prudent diggers on the Ballarat fields repaired to the Gold Office (below) next to the Colonial Bank in Lydiard Street. There the gold was weighed (right) and purchased, after which it was taken under armed escort to Melbourne. During the early days of the gold rushes the precious metal was used as currency. The digger would hand over his pouch of dust to the storekeeper who sold him goods, often at vastly inflated prices, in return. The scales (left) are in the reconstructed offices of Carver and Dalton, auctioneers, Sovereign Hill. Below, left: Commercial Bank of Australia, Swan Hill Folk Museum.

Thomas and Richard Clarke kept a store on Main Road, Ballarat, next to the *Times* office. It provided most of the diggers' needs, from simple utensils to food: tea, sugar, bacon, cheese etc. The interior at far right, with its sawdust-strewn floor, shows the ornate coffee-grinder and, on the wall behind it, a jar of colza oil, used as a fuel before kerosene. An advertisement on the wall offers ice which was imported from Lake Wenham, near Boston, America. The ice was carried in the hulls of sailing vessels, packed in sawdust and wood shavings, then brought overland to cool the drinks of thirsty diggers during the Ballarat summer. Below, right: The counter, with cupboards and drawers of groceries. Below: Ballarat's New York Bakery also served lamb hotpot, roast beef and apple pie.

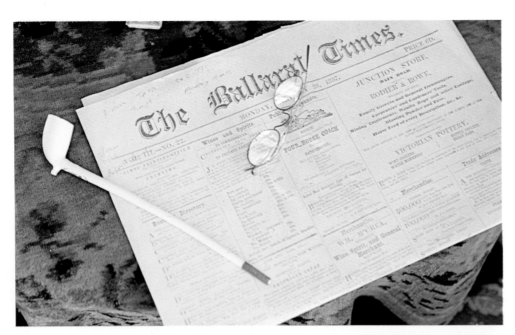

The *Ballarat Times* was the diggers' newspaper, a voice of popular dissent on the goldfields. Its editor, Henry Seekamp, was gaoled for sedition at the time of the Eureka Stockade and gained further notoriety when Lola Montez the Irish adventuress and dancer horsewhipped him through the bar of the United States Hotel for remarks published in the *Times*. The Albion Improved Press (below, left) dates from the 1860s. Right: Chandler and Price hand platen of a later period at the *Times* office, Sovereign Hill.

By the 1860s the relatively shallow shafts of the early Ballarat East alluvial diggings had been worked out. The gold was still there but it lay deep and encased in quartz. To extract it required engineering skill and considerable capital investment. The Sovereign Hill Quartz Mining Company, formed in 1868, was one of many working the deep leads by shafts and underground tunnels. The poppet head of the mine is an accurate reconstruction built on the site of the North Normanby mine on the south channel of the Red Hill Gully lead. The soft slate and bedrock excavated from the mine was tipped on to the mullock heap beside the poppet head. Above: Entrance to main tunnel.

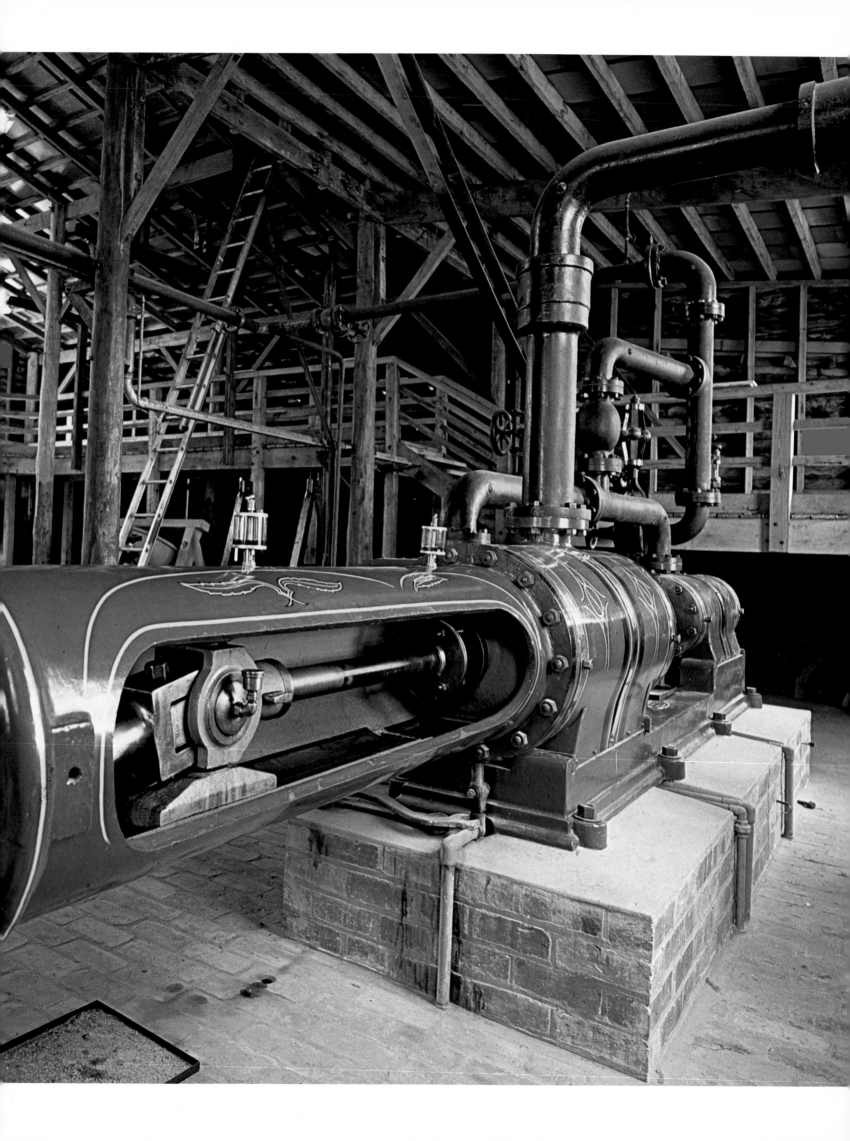

Gold-bearing quartz from the mine was crushed in the battery to extract the gold. The 10-head stamper battery at Sovereign Hill (above) is driven by a tandem compound steam engine (right) manufactured at the Phoenix Foundry, Ballarat. Each hammer of the battery weighs 386 kilograms. The engine house stood beside the poppet head and housed a wood-fired furnace heating a boiler which supplied the mine's winding engine. The drums of the engine raised or lowered cables attached to the cages in the mine's shaft, while a compressor forced fresh air to the working faces below ground. The engine house also contained the miners' changing quarters.

Over page: Sovereign Hill Historical Park on the site of the old Ballarat East goldfields covers, in part, leases of the original Sovereign quartz mine, the Speedwell and Normanby North companies. The diggings re-create the decade from 1851; the mining complex spans fifty years.

The majority of the gold-diggers were British; a number came from America but they were greatly outnumbered by the Chinese. On the goldfields the Chinese lived in their own communities and most often worked over claims and mullock-heaps abandoned by European miners. Racial prejudice, combined with resentment at their working methods, caused several disturbances during the 1850s and 1870s, notably at Bendigo; Lambing Flat, New South Wales; and Clunes, Victoria. Right: The Joss House at Emu Point, Bendigo, was probably built in the 1860s. It was called by the local Chinese the Big Gold Mountain Temple and the main altar (pictured) was for the worship of the god Kwan Gung. Left: Modern re-creation of a typical goldfields joss house at Sovereign Hill. Below: Chinese cemetery, prayer desk and burning towers at Beechworth, Victoria.

124

Beechworth, Victoria, was once the principal town of the Ovens River goldfields. Gold was first found there in 1852 and it became one of the richest goldfields of Australia over the next ten years, during which time it yielded 116 650 279 grams. Much of this passed through the Sub-Treasury and Gold Office (far left). This building (now the police station) stands next to the Court House where the bushranger Ned Kelly twice stood trial. On the far right of the picture is the verandah of the District Survey Office. The three were built between 1857 and 1860. Above: Cast-iron lace verandah frames the Post Office, Beechworth.

126

As the gold rushes slowed and ceased towns that had sprung up prematurely withered and died. In 1872 Hill End, New South Wales, saw the greatest gold rush in the colony's history. The town had nearly two kilometres of shops including 28 hotels; it produced the gargantuan Holtermann nugget one-and-a-half metres high. But in 1874 yields fell sharply. The diggers moved out and the weeds moved in. Left: The Coffee Palace. Above, right: Remains of Pullen's Battery. Above: 1850 building and shop, Carcoa, New South Wales. Right: Remains of Ovens Goldfields Hospital (1856) at Beechworth.

In 1876 Walter Lindesay Richardson, one of the thousands who had failed to make a fortune on the Victorian goldfields, settled in the town of Chiltern. Gold had made the town rich but Richardson this time wisely stayed with his first vocation: medicine. Years later his daughter Ethel wrote fondly of their home 'Lake View' (above): 'I liked it because all its windows were french windows and usually stood wide open ... and because it had a verandah running round three sides'. Ethel became famous as Henry Handel Richardson and 'Lake View' as the setting of *Ultima Thule* in the great trilogy in which her father appeared as the tragic central character: *The Fortunes of Richard Mahony*. Far right: The kitchen, 'Lake View'. Right: The drawing room.

An American, Freeman Cobb, heard of the Victorian gold rush while working for a coaching company in Massachusetts He decided to come to Australia and, on the ship out, met three other young men with whom he subsequently formed the firm of Cobb & Co. Their first coaches were imported from America and featured the leather thorough-braces or 'springs' which gave a more comfortable ride. The partners sold out after two years but Cobb & Co. went on to become part of Australian history. Right: Bath's stables and Cobb & Co. offices as they were c. 1854 in Lydiard Street, Ballarat, at Sovereign Hill.

As the gold rush was dying in Victoria in the 1860s a new, lesser rush was beginning in South Australia. Copper had been discovered at Burra Burra in 1845 and a large community of Cornishmen had begun mines. Development slowed during the gold rushes but in 1860 and 1861 important new discoveries were made at Wallaroo and Moonta respectively on the Yorke Peninsula. Left: Ruins of Hughes Pump House, Moonta. Right; below, left: Ruins of mine buildings at Burra. Below, right: Miner's underground house, Burra. As many as 2000 miners lived in underground dugouts in the banks of the Burra Creek.

The Cornish miners at Moonta built neat, cosy cottages with most of the domestic comforts. Right: Dining room of cottage built in 1870 by brickmaker John Wood. The exterior walls are of limestone, with bricks around corners, windows, doors, fireplaces and chimneys. The floors were originally of firmed earth covered by mats or by goat or kangaroo skins. Below, left: The parlour, with the miner's rocking chair. Below: Stone cottage of Cornish miner's family at Willunga, south of Adelaide, where the Cornishmen worked the quarries to produce slate for roofing and flooring.

Explorers

'... *the colonists dreamed that one day they would discover an inland sea, a "new Mediterranean" in the centre of the continent.*'

ALAN MOOREHEAD, *Cooper's Creek*

The settlements of Sydney, Melbourne, Adelaide and Brisbane with their satellite townships were no more than tiny specks on a continent the size of the United States, two-thirds the size of Europe. For all the broughams bowling down Collins Street, the ladies in crinolines and the champagne being drunk at the balls in the Exhibition Hall, they were living in a little capsule, encompassed by a huge unknown wilderness, they were suspended, as it were, in space. If they stepped outside the capsule they were lost.

The coastline of the continent had been charted from the sea, but as yet very few adventurers had penetrated far into the interior. All that was known was that the further one advanced into that vast empty space the hotter and drier it became, and it was perhaps because of this aridity that the colonists dreamed that one day they would discover an inland sea, a 'new Mediterranean' in the centre of the continent. It was like the legendary Atlantis or the land of Prester John; the more serious geographers scouted the idea, yet it had the persistence of a mystery. After all, no one had actually been in the centre, no one could say with finality exactly what was to be found there, and the fact that half a dozen expeditions had already set out to resolve the matter and had returned defeated seemed, irrationally, to suggest that some great prize was awaiting the first explorer who succeeded in breaking through.

The notion of an inland sea arose from the fact that the mountains so far discovered lay on the eastern seaboard and all the principal rivers, the Murray, the Darling, and the Murrumbidgee, flowed inland from these mountains towards the west; and in the west lay the tremendous unexplored tract, an area some 2600 kilometres long by 1300 kilometres wide, bounded by the 20th and 32nd degrees of latitude and the 115th and 140th degrees of longitude: an area more than half the size of Europe.

A good deal was already known about the interior, of course, through the travels of the early explorers, and one man in particular had shown the way ahead. Charles Sturt is something of a giant in Australian exploration, and indeed of exploration anywhere, and it is strange that his name is not better known, since he was the most literate of travellers, the most persistent and the most adventurous. Like so many other remarkable Englishmen of the nineteenth century, Sturt was born in India and at an early age sent back to England to be educated, first at Harrow and then in the army. By 1814, when he was nineteen, he had already served with Wellington against the French in the Peninsular War, and with the British in Canada against the Americans. After Waterloo he returned to garrison duty in France, and when his regiment was transferred to Ireland he was involved in the famine riots of 1821–22. In 1823 he was gazetted a lieutenant and two years later a captain. He was then sent out to New South Wales in charge of a convict guard.

Already in 1827 Sydney was an established settlement with cornfields and orchards running down to the sea, and it was not unusual to see forty or fifty sailing-ships in the harbour. But in 1828 a drought set in, and with the failure of the crops the settlers began to look towards the regions behind the coastal mountains, where they hoped they would find more fertile land. Sturt got in with a group of young men whose names were soon to become famous as explorers — Mitchell, Hume and others — all eager to find the 'new Australian Caspian Sea', and in 1828 he led his own party inland. With six convicts to carry the baggage he followed the Macquarie River to the point where, among swamps, it entered a large westward-flowing stream, which he named after his patron the Darling. A year later he set out again, turning southwards this time to the Murrumbidgee, and with a boat he had carried overland he sailed downstream until he reached a still more important river, the Murray, and this he followed to its junction with the Darling and then to its outlet at Lake Alexandrina, on the southern ocean.

This prodigious journey of over 3200 kilometres illuminated the whole river system of the south, and earned for Sturt much praise in Sydney, and a grant of land. It also undermined his health, and for the time being ruined his eyesight. For the next ten years he was obliged to stick to his farm and administrative duties in Norfolk Island and New South Wales, and in 1839 he was appointed surveyor-general in Adelaide. But he did not like a sedentary life, and repeatedly offered himself for new expeditions. He was still dreaming of an inland sea. 'I have a strange idea,' he wrote, 'that there may be a central sea not far from the Darling in latitude 29° and I should go prepared for a *voyage*.'

In 1844 at last the authorities let him go. He was now 49, but his eyesight had improved and he was still physically robust. The party that assembled in Adelaide that winter was exceptionally strong: 16 men, 11 horses, 30 bullocks, 200 sheep (to be eaten on the way), a boat, a couple of heavy carts and a year's provisions. The expedition's draughtsman was a wiry little Scots officer, 168 centimetres high and under 57 kilograms in weight, named John McDouall Stuart, and among those who came to see them off was a particular friend of Sturt's, Charles Cooper, a lawyer who was subsequently to become the first chief justice of South Australia. A farewell breakfast was given for the expedition by the colonists, and then Sturt, with a straw hat on his head and mounted on Duncan, his old grey horse, led the way out of town. They marched first to the Murray River, and followed it up-stream to the confluence with the Darling. About 290 kilometres up the Darling they reached Lake Cawndilla near the little outpost of Menindie, and here, having built a stockade, they turned north-westwards into the unknown.

Had they known it, Sturt and his men were marching into one of the most appalling summers ever recorded. The end of 1844 found them still toiling slowly northward — a Biblical-looking group with their ox-carts and their flock of sheep — and early in 1845 they reached the 29th latitude. Here they stuck on a waterhole for six months while the land dried up around them, unable either to go forward or to go back until rain fell.

The extreme temperatures of the centre are very bearable because of the dryness of the air, but even so the heat this year was unbelievable. It rose to 132 degrees in the shade and 157 degrees in the sun. It penetrated to a depth of up to 120 centimetres into the ground, it forced the screws out of wooden boxes and horn combs split into fine laminae. The men's hair ceased to grow and their finger nails became as brittle as glass. Sturt found it almost impossible to write his diary; the lead dropped out of his pencils when he picked them up, and when he used a pen the ink dried as it touched the paper.

By April it was a little cooler, and thunder clouds began to bank up on the

Preceding pages: The gibber-strewn wastes of Sturt's Stony Desert which lies between Cooper Creek and the Diamantina River in north-east South Australia. Time-after-time Charles Sturt's attempts to locate a 'great inland sea' brought him to the edge of this desolate region which he first traversed in 1845. On its rocky perimeters Sturt's hopes of finding the living heart of the Australian continent perished.

horizon. At last on July 12 a gentle but persistent rain started to fall, and after a few days it developed into a downpour. Now they had floods to contend with, cold nights and even frost, but at least they could move, and as a guarantee that life was returning to the parched earth, swans and ducks and other migrating birds began to reappear. Sturt sent some of his men back to Adelaide and with the remainder pushed on to the north-west. At a place which he named Fort Grey, close to the extreme north-western corner of New South Wales, he formed another base where he dropped off more of his men, while he himself and a young companion named John Harris-Browne pushed on again, taking fifteen weeks' provisions with them. They reached and named the Strzelecki Creek, and then followed it northward until they entered a region where the horses' hooves were cut by flint-like stones and left no track. Here on every side there were 'stupendous and almost insurmountable sand-ridges of a fiery red'. These ridges, Sturt went on, 'like headlands projecting into the sea, abutted upon an immense plain where, but for a line of low trees far to the north-east, and one bright red sandhill shining in the sunlight, not a feature broke the dead level, the gloomy purple hue . . .' He named this region the Stony Desert. Beyond it there were glimpses of the 'better country' for which he was searching, but presently he was again among sand dunes, and at the end of August, on latitude 25 and longitude 139, he gave up all hope of finding his inland sea in that direction.

They found their way back through the red sand-ridges with white clay pans lying in between and the cloudless sky overhead — a country of red, white and blue. If they had not quite reached the centre, at least they had been almost half-way across the continent, and they had gone further than any other man. Both horses and men looked like skeletons when they reached Fort Grey at the end of seven weeks. They had ridden nearly 1450 kilometres. It was now October 1845 and they had heard nothing from the outside world since they had left Adelaide fourteen months before.

After the briefest of rests Sturt set out for the north once more, taking with him this time his draughtsman McDouall Stuart and two men named Mack and Morgan. They had four riding-horses and four pack-horses, and once again they expected to be out for several months. Harris-Browne was left in charge at Fort Grey, and before setting out Sturt gave him instructions that he was only to retire from the place if his supply of water failed or his men fell ill. In that event he was to leave a message saying where he had gone, and this message was to be placed in a bottle and buried under a tree which they chose together.

His hopes for an inland sea had revived, and it was a bitter disappointment when once again they struck the Stony Desert. 'Coming suddenly on it,' Sturt recorded, 'I almost lost my breath. If anything it looked more forbidding than before. Herbless and treeless it filled more than half the horizon. Not an object was visible on which to steer, yet we held on to our course by compass like a ship at sea.'

A few days later, when they were 190 kilometres upstream from their original starting-point, they came on a crowd of some 400 blacks, more than they had ever seen before. The men were very fine, no tribal scars on their bodies, no bulging stomachs among them, and no missing teeth. They were very friendly once they got over their fear of the horses. They came forward with gifts of ducks and flour-cakes, and held up troughs of water for the horses to drink. But they also blasted Sturt's hopes for the last time: from this point on they said the stream diminished, and nothing lay further to the east but the desert. Riding out in that direction Sturt came on a swamp, and beyond this he was confronted by an endless plain.

Now finally he had had enough, and the party turned homeward. They retraced their steps down the creek to the point where they had first reached it, and then struck out for Fort Grey and the south. Sturt wrote: 'Before we finally left the neighbourhood where our hopes had been so often raised and depressed, I gave the name of Cooper's Creek to the fine watercourse we had so anxiously traced, as a proof of my respect for Mr Cooper, the judge of South Australia.'

Sturt never managed to return to the centre. His eyes began to trouble him again, and in 1853 he returned to England and died there sixteen years later. But his discoveries had opened a vast new field for exploration. From every side men began to push into the interior. Thomas Livingstone Mitchell, the New South Wales surveyor-general, struck inland from Sydney on a series of journeys and discovered the Victoria River. Later his assistant Kennedy traced the Victoria downstream and found that it linked up with Cooper's Creek. Meanwhile Ludwig Leichhardt, a German botanist, travelled across the tropical north of the continent as far as Port Essington. In 1848 he set out once more from the east coast with the idea of crossing the continent to Perth, and was never heard of again.

Leichhardt's disappearance caused a great stir at the time — for years afterwards there were stories of a wild white man roaming in the interior — and Augustus Charles Gregory, the Queensland surveyor-general, made two separate expeditions to find him. In the course of these journeys Gregory also followed the Cooper, and he eventually succeeded in reaching Mount Hopeless in South Australia, thus linking up his own researches with those of Sturt and Eyre some twenty years earlier. Then in 1853 a resourceful character named Captain Francis Cadell got a small steamer over the bar at the mouth of the Murray and sailed upstream as far as Swan Hill and back.

Finally there was Sturt's draughtsman, John McDouall Stuart, and he was proving himself to be the most persistent traveller of them all. After the 1844 expedition he made several journeys to the north of Adelaide, and in March 1860 he was preparing to set out again for the centre of the continent.

Yet still the basic objects eluded them all. North of Sturt's furthest, on latitude 25, it was still *terra incognita*. Was it possible for a party to cross the continent from south to north? It was not merely curiosity that was involved in this, the persistent urge for men to go where no one else had ever been before. In 1860 the settlements in the south were still divided from Britain and Europe by a two months' sea voyage, and the introduction of steam had not materially speeded up communications. What if you could build a telegraph line from Adelaide to the northern coast and there link up with the cable that already extended through India to south-east Asia? That was a compelling idea. If realized it would mean that instead of waiting four months you could communicate with London in a few hours. There was also the possibility of opening up trade with south-east Asia through a port on the north coast. Then of course there was the hunger for land itself: all of it free, unused, waiting there for the first-comers to take possession. One would have thought that Sturt's hardships were enough to disabuse anyone of such optimistic dreams as these, but here, as in the Sahara, mirages floated on the horizon and oases like Cooper's Creek were a promise that they could be real.

On 27 January, 1845, Charles Sturt and his party, stumbling through the searing inland summer in their quest for the great inland sea, found rest and water at a spot they named Depot Glen (above), near the present settlement of Milparinka in north-western New South Wales. Here they were to remain for nearly six months while every watercourse around them dried up in the ferocious drought and the temperature seldom fell below 38 degrees Celsius. When steady rain came on 12 July Sturt sent a party, which included his second-in-command James Poole, off to Adelaide for supplies. They had barely left before Poole was dead. They brought him back to Depot Glen and buried him beneath a Grevillea (left). Sturt pressed on northwards.

Sturt had shown that there was no 'great inland sea'. But whatever lay beyond the northernmost point of his exploration remained a mystery. This riddle of the interior bred an irrepressible desire to know the truth; it culminated in the most ambitious of all the journeys of Australian exploration: a planned crossing of the continent from south to north; at last the nature of Australia's heartland would be revealed. The expedition was commanded by Robert O'Hara Burke, the former police inspector at Castlemaine, Victoria. His second-in-command was to be a young surveyor, William John Wills. In August 1860 the expedition set off from Melbourne with 18 men and 25 camels. Leaving depots along the way at Menindee and Cooper Creek, Burke and Wills, together with their companions Gray and King, pushed across the length of the continent to reach their goal, the shores of the Gulf of Carpentaria, in February 1861. The journey left them critically weakened by fatigue and malnutrition. On the return trip to the Cooper Creek depot Gray died and Burke, Wills and King were near collapse. On 21 April 1861 they staggered into the depot clearing to find a Coolibah tree (right) freshly blazed with the message: 'DIG 3 ft N.W.' Beneath the tree the explorers found a note which revealed that a support party had left the site less than eight hours before, after having waited for them for eighteen weeks. Shocked and depressed, the explorers made desperate efforts to press on, but lassitude and lack of water prevented them from getting far from the creek. On 27 June Wills wrote a last letter to his father; two days later, at 8 a.m. Burke joined him in death. Only John King survived to tell the true story of the inland.

Tranquil waters of Cooper Creek (below) at Burke and Wills' depot. The carving of Robert O'Hara Burke on the Dig Tree was made in 1898. Below, right: Tree blazed by the expedition at Menindee. Bottom, right: Mark left by the expedition at Paine's Hotel, Menindee, where Burke and Wills spent spent the night.

Over page: a decade after Burke and Wills died, Charles Todd, Postmaster-General of South Australia, led a party which laid a telegraph line across the continent from Port Augusta, South Australia, to Darwin, where it joined a submarine cable linking Australia with Europe and Asia. The old Telegraph Office (pictured) at Tennant Creek, Northern Territory, still stands.

On the Land

'When their wandering urge had been satiated many became possessed of the dream of settling down happily on the land.'

MICHAEL CANNON, *Life in the Country*

The selectors' rush to the land superficially resembled that of the early squatters. Their bark huts were built in much the same way, at least until late in the century when the widespread use of galvanised iron and mill-sawn timber altered their external appearance. Inside these primitive homes, living conditions were often just as dirty and uncomfortable as those endured by the squatting pioneers. But the squatters had been playing for major stakes — large annual profits from wool and ultimate ownership of large tracts of land — and usually had not dragged women and children into the miseries of pioneering life. By comparison, the selectors' prospects were as mean as the penny-pinching methods they were forced to impose on themselves and their families. The human products of these contrasting situations — separated by only twenty or thirty years in time — were so different that they formed two opposing groups at the very top and the very bottom of the social scale.

Many selectors came from the classes of immigrant gold-seekers and itinerant rural workers. When their wandering urge had been satiated, many became possessed by the dream of settling down happily on the land. This urge to own a manageable bit of soil, rather than endless acres of pasture, was the great 'Australian Dream' of the nineteenth century, and has still not quite faded from the popular imagination.

Having won the right to occupy a block somewhere, the selector went shopping for his minimum requirements: a horse and dray; a single-furrow plough and harrow to be pulled by the same long-suffering horse; a few bags of seed; axes, saws, spades and fencing tools; the usual simple bush rations; and a few pots and pans. As selectors moved with these frugal possessions towards their land they reminded one onlooker of 'scenes described in the Old Testament, when patriarchs moved in search of fresh pastures accompanied by their descendants'. First came the drays, 'with occasionally a tilted cart containing the younger members of a family', then a few pigs, sheep, cows or goats, often followed by 'a female or two on side saddles, and some thriving male cornstalks'.

But they rarely profited by the earlier man's experiences. Most selectors, and politicians for that matter, seriously under-estimated the amount of capital required. Farmers and their families clung to the dream that once they had bred a few more animals and paid one or two instalments on the land, the products of the soil would not only support them but provide sufficient surplus for future payments, interest, improvements, and even expansion. This fallacy, encouraged by successive land acts in all states, led to an amount of loss and suffering we can only guess at today.

A couple of hundred pounds in savings was simply not enough to enable most selectors to survive. Many were compelled to borrow money to continue their ventures. Until the end of the century, when reality forced its way through, finance was not widely available from banks or government: the selectors generally had to pay extortionate interest rates to private lenders. These lenders (whose real purpose only too often was to seize the land after the hardest work had been done) used the rationalisation that lending to selectors was a risky business. So it was, but the interest rates were often the final straw which broke men who would otherwise have made good farmers.

One squatter, William Lewis of Stoneleigh (Vic.), lent money to selectors at 20 per cent interest, forcing them to sign a reconveyance before handing over the money. He thought that in five years time they would be glad to take

2s. an acre and leave the district. J. A. Buchanan, Wimmera valuer, told a Royal Commission that selectors in that shire were paying at least 22½ per cent to local storekeepers. R. W. Bennett, a Horsham merchant, admitted that his average rate of interest was 35 per cent.

Many storekeepers made large profits by bartering the selectors' farm produce against cash loans, deducting up to 70 per cent of the true value. Other merchants arranged to send the selectors' produce to market in their own name, allowing accounts to run up until the goods were sold. In a famous autobiographical passage, 'Steele Rudd' described how a storekeeper sold his father's first harvest of corn for £12, then deducted the grocery account which had swollen to £9: 'Dad was speechless, and looked sick . . . went home and sat on a block and stared into the fire . . .' There was not much to be said in favour of the shopkeeper mentality which battened on the desperation of struggling farmers.

Most under-capitalised selectors were forced to eke out their resources by searching for part-time jobs in the area while their families tried to cope with the work of the farm. The squatter might fight them for the land, but he also unwittingly carried some through to success by employing them as shearers and rouseabouts.

As in their goldfield days, many selectors and their families lived in tents until they had time to build a hut. The first essential was to secure a reliable water supply. Unless the farm bordered a permanent creek, which was not always possible, the selector had to dig a dam for his animals and a well for the household supply. Clay had to be found and bricks baked to line the well: where this material was scarce the sides were sometimes formed of closely-fitted timbers.

From the tent the selector usually moved to a bark or log hut built by himself. Many nineteenth century farmers remained at this stage until they died. An observer of the Wimmera in the late 1880s gave a picture which could be applied to almost any crop-growing selection of the time: the usual homestead was 'a poor congeries of sheds, with one mud chimney very much out of the perpendicular'. Although recently built, many seemed 'crumbling to decay'. There were 'no vegetables growing — nor so much as a gooseberry bush, a marigold, or a daisy'. And this observer had set out with the intention of writing a glowing picture of the nation's progress!

The sketch of selectors' living conditions given by Henry Lawson in his story 'Water Them Geraniums' was strictly factual: rough slab furniture rooted in the muddy floor, tins spread about to catch leaks from the roof, beds made from poles and flour bags, a ragged patchwork quilt spread over the parents' bed, kerosene tins used as saucepans, and so on. During the night dried cowdung smouldered on the fire to keep mosquitoes at bay. On a rough mantelpiece rested a few pathetic ornaments from an almost-forgotten earlier life. Progress from this low state was a definite sign of success, for glazed windows, iron roofs, and smooth timbered walls and floors all cost hard cash.

As in the case of squatters' wives, selectors' wives included women who had survived the worst that the gold diggings could offer, female immigrants from Britain who arrived in large numbers after shipping conditions improved in the 1860s, and the wives of town artisans who had decided to take up

Preceding pages: Southampton homestead at Greenbushes, Western Australia.

farming. Lonely grinding poverty, usually on the very edge of bankruptcy, was their common lot, with the monotonous drudgery relieved only by an occasional visit from a neighbour or travelling hawker.

The amount of sheer physical labour these women had to get through each day was enormous. First there was the problem of providing from meagre resources three substantial meals a day for the rest of the family. The heavy manual work of the farm had to be kept going at all costs: if food was short the mother went without. Corn-meal, damper, vegetables and eggs were the best that most selectors' families could expect. Native animals were killed wherever possible for their meat, the slaughter of a sheep or pig being reserved for the rarest of festive occasions (unless one of the squatter's animals happened to 'stray' on to the selection). Later in the century the rapid spread of rabbits may have destroyed many squatters' hopes, but the meat saved numerous selectors' families from actual starvation.

Around the hut the women and children were always responsible for the garden and fruit trees they may have hopefully planted. More important to the farm economy was the work of tending fowls and milking cows. In moderate weather that might seem a pleasant enough occupation, but Henry Lawson could never forget those 'smothering hot mornings' when the heaps of manure had turned to fine dust, in the midst of which the housewife had to bail up and milk 'cranky old cows', haul at young steers that were too strong for her, hump great buckets of sour milk to the pigs and poddy (hand-fed) calves. In winter, on those 'bitter black rainy mornings', she trudged ankle-deep in 'black liquid filth' wearing old boots and 'maybe a three-bushel bag over her shoulders'. During times of drought she climbed she-oaks and apple trees, 'awkwardly lopping off boughs to feed the starving cattle'.

Such activities were universally regarded as women's work: even in 1946 more than half the wives on Wimmera farms still milked the cows, and nearly three-quarters had sole responsibility for the fowls. They still drove to town once a week, as their ancestors had done seventy years earlier, to sell eggs, butter and cream for their 'pin money'. Only the roads had improved. Back in 1870, farmers' wives with produce to sell at the town of Green Swamp (NSW) had to wade up to their waists across the Macintyre River until a footbridge could be built.

Since the farmer could rarely afford to hire labour, he relied on breeding a large family to relieve his physical burdens. To the wife's other problems, therefore, must be added the fact that she was practically always pregnant or nursing new babies, often in filthy conditions which meant that half of them died and the effort had been wasted to that extent. Breeding of farm animals was carried out more efficiently than that. Nevertheless, some very large families survived. In the healthier climate of the Darling Downs, for instance, six selectors could boast of seventy-six living children between them, an average of thirteen per family. Some exceptional mothers in the area bore eighteen living children.

While the woman gave birth in her rough bed, assisted — if she was fortunate — by an experienced neighbour, the husband managed to conceal any anxiety he may have felt. Rarely was there any thought of fetching a doctor: that would have cost money. When one of Henry Cox's children was due, he thought he had better ride home from a distant ploughing job. Unfortunately it was raining, and he only reached Natimuk (Vic.), writing laconically, 'It was fine the next day, and I got home all right, although late, and found mother and son doing remarkably well. The rain, however, had soaked through the house. I dug a furrow round the back and sides, and that fixed it.' Another settler lived with his wife and baby beneath their bullock wagon until they built a hut. The baby's diet 'was for the most part sago made with water, with a little goat's milk' donated by a neighbour.

Children were put to work from the earliest possible age, collecting firewood, gathering eggs, minding new babies, driving stock to water, breaking up clods left after harrowing the fields, sowing seed, acting as scarecrows, picking up mail, digging the garden, and so on. Every selector's child had to take his turn at milking: 'to be kicked out of bed at four in the morning to milk cows, and to be kicked right through the day till nine and ten o'clock at night doing this, that and everything . . .' Henry Lawson's experience was fairly typical. Every day he had to milk half a dozen cows, then ride a horse five miles to school at Mudgee (NSW). When he was thirteen years old, the cows caught pleuro-pneumonia, Lawson recording that he 'used to bleed them by cutting their tails and ears in the sickening heat — and was often sick over the job — and inoculate them with a big needle . . .'

Such children received only a few years intermittent education at best. Lawson, for instance, went to school for only three years and remained unable to spell properly throughout his life. Even when primary education became compulsory from the 1870s on, the children were usually kept away during harvest time by a variety of pretexts.

As the sons grew older many continued to toil on without wages, on the unwritten understanding that one day they could inherit the farm. If the property was not an expanding one, which was the usual story, younger sons could only look forward to joining the itinerant labour force or going to work in town or city. This pattern continued well into the present century: in 1946 more than 80 per cent of wheat farmers were the sons of wheat farmers. Only half had been paid any wages during their life, and even these received only a few shillings 'pocket money' on reaching their twenties.

The picture was not wholly grim for selectors' children, however. There were wonderful compensations in the fresh outdoor life, compared with the grimy surroundings of city children. They could creep away from the hut and indulge in the delights of fishing, birds-nesting, and swimming. 'Steele Rudd' wrote that he cherished memories of his childhood selection life for 'its freedom, its joys, its careless hopes and sorrows, its utter irresponsibility'. On Sundays, the traditional day of family relaxation (except that the cows still had to be milked), life was often more rewarding on the little farm by the very fact of its isolation and dependence of all members of the family on one another. Even father might relax and play cricket.

Nor was the mother's lot entirely hopeless. In the quietness of the bush, with children content with the simplest satisfactions, there was a freedom from the stress and alienation of most urban living. The frequency of hardship made neighbourly assistance an everyday reality, even to the extent that when one parent died other selectors would make time in their busy lives to 'see the family through' by harvesting the crop, preparing the meals, and so on. Once accepted into the ranks of a farming community, selectors achieved a degree of social security which contrasted greatly with the sufferings of anonymous city workers hit by hard times.

Gulf station, north-east of Yarra Glen, Victoria, was built by Scottish settler William Bell in 1854. Bell, who had been a builder in Melbourne and who had cut timber in the Diamond Creek area, built his homestead of local gums and stringybarks. The frames and supports were of whole logs or tree trunks with the bark removed; the walls were of palings split by hand, weatherboard, or adzed slabs. The former kitchen, with its verandah (left) has walls of vertical slabs. Above: The Butcher's shop. Right: Entrance.

Working with only saw and adze, the pioneers performed herculean tasks. Cutting large timber was a two-man job done in a saw pit. The 'top-notcher', standing above the log, did the hardest work, while the man below was showered with sawdust. Planks and wall slabs were cut in this arduous way from logs of considerable diameter. The settler's hut (far left) at the Earlystreet village, Brisbane, has vertical slab walls. Large saws used in cutting timber are on the walls. Above: Cattle fence of split saplings at Tambaroora, New South Wales, is 150 years old. Left: Pioneer's abandoned shack of timber slabs, with wooden shingle roof, in the Hunter Valley.

'Glenmore' homestead at Rockhampton, Queensland, was commenced in 1858. In that year gold was discovered on the property 'Canoona', setting off a rush which led to the establishment of the town. The first hut on the property was built of logs held together with dowling, by J. Arthur Macarthy. The only openings were the door and the window aperture (above) which could be used for defence. Far left: The entrance to 'Glenmore', showing the vertical slab walls and heavy timber flooring. Left: Family relics at 'Glenmore'.

Scottish settlers Andrew and Peter Beveridge drove their cattle to the lower Murray area near Swan Hill in 1846. They camped at a spot where Major Thomas Mitchell, the Surveyor-General, had rested ten years earlier, looked around the district and chose a spot nearby for their property 'Tyntynder'. They built the homestead of straight, clean-stemmed Murray pine. The walls were of logs laid horizontally between posts, the roof of bark, and the doors and shutters were fashioned from hides stretched over sapling frames. A few years later they veneered their walls with hand-made bricks and gradually added to the house. 'Tyntynder' provided a strategic resting-place for travellers, and the pine-walled dining room (above) welcomed such notable guests as Baron von Mueller, Captain Francis Cadell and the explorers Burke and Wills.

'Para Para' homestead near Gawler, South Australia, was completed in 1862 by wealthy miller Walter Duffield. The house took ten years to build and was lavishly appointed. The walls and cornices of the dining room (left) which appear to be papered are, in fact, painted by hand. The lower walls consisted of wooden panels (below, left) painted with foliage or fruit. The polished doors (right) were similarly embellished.

As many as 4000 people at a time attended parties held in spacious grounds which included orchards, vineyards, an apiary, 180 varieties of roses and 10 000 orange trees.

In 1890 Cordillo Downs station on the edge of Sturt's Stony Desert in far north-east South Australia, shore 85 000 sheep and produced 1000 bales of scoured wool. One of a chain of stations owned by Sir Thomas Elder and his partners, it was first leased in 1878 but development did not begin until 1883 when the great shearing shed (left; right) was built. The curved roofs were adopted to save timber. Below: The Store. Above: Thatched verandahs around the meat house.

John Macarthur planted Australia's first vines in 1820 but Prussian and Silesian migrants to South Australia in the 1830s were the pioneer vignerons. Johan Seppelt, who left Germany in 1849, established his winery (top left) in the Barossa Valley where his original recipes and essences (below, left) are still kept. Right: Chateau Tahbilk winery at Nagambie, Victoria, was built in 1860. Below: Yalumba winery, Angaston, South Australia. Bottom: 1880 cart for grape skins, Seppeltsfield.

William Shoobridge planted the first hops in Tasmania in 1823 and pioneered one of the colony's most important industries. More than 40 years later his son Ebenezer acquired Bushy Park (right; below), 19 kilometres upstream from New Norfolk in the fertile Derwent Valley. Here techniques invented by his father made it the biggest and most successful hop field in the southern hemisphere. Left: Old oast house, Macquarie Plains. Below, right: Old hop baling press, New Norfolk.

Machine-cut weatherboards gained sudden popularity in the years following the gold rushes and soon became the universal economic timber cladding. Their insulating properties, when used in double-wall construction, were also vastly superior to those of iron. In the 1870s English mills perfected corrugated iron, and the timber-framed, iron-roofed house came to dominate the architecture of the Australian bush. Far left: Old farm building at 'Camden Park'. Above: Humble dwelling at Murrurundi, New South Wales. Left: House at Gympie, Queensland.

Early settlers' graves near
Gordon in the Flinders Ranges,
South Australia.

Nationhood

'It was the time to cherish the good life — a time for joy and contentment, an Indian Summer for reflection.'

R M YOUNGER, *March to Nationhood*

No. 1.]

Vi

W

is enac

declare

Year a

Queens

Austra

wealth

Commonwealth of Australia

Gazette.

PUBLISHED BY AUTHORITY.

TUESDAY, 1 JANUARY.   **[1901.**

By the QUEEN.

A PROCLAMATION.

RIA R.

REAS by an Act of Parliament passed in the Sixty-third and Sixty-fourth Years Our Reign intituled, "An Act to constitute the Commonwealth of *Australia*," it that it shall be lawful for the Queen, with the advice of the Privy Council, to Proclamation, that, on and after a day therein appointed, not being later than One the passing of this Act, the people of *New South Wales, Victoria, South Australia,* d, and *Tasmania*, and also, if Her Majesty is satisfied that the people of *Western* have agreed thereto, of *Western Australia*, shall be united in a Federal Common- der the name of the Commonwealth of Australia.

d whereas We are satisfied that the people of *Western Australia* have agreed thereto

A few days before 1900 closed a reassuring announcement was made in Sydney: the champagne ordered by the Government of New South Wales had come safely to hand and had been stored in large stacks in passages and rooms at Parliament House in readiness for the government's round of commemorative picnics and banquets. The first of these, the State Banquet in the Sydney Town Hall, was greeted by the Press as Australia's 'most brilliant assemblage ever under one roof'; it included nearly all the country's prominent politicians, lawyers, and officials.

By this time Sydney was in joyous midsummer mood. 'The city has put on her carnival costume of many colours,' wrote Oriel, a special writer of the Melbourne *Argus* touring the harbour city, whose observations were published on 31 December 1900. Oriel wrote: 'The old century is dying amidst strange scenes in Sydney. Train after train has been discharging its freight of tired passengers from every inland town. Steamship after steamship has landed her load of sightseers from every part of Australia and from many parts of the older world, until the city is hardly able to contain the crowds, which overflow into harbour steamers, and are poured out from the heights above Watson's Bay, the long expanse of the beach at Manly, and all the innumerable nooks and corners of Port Jackson. In Sydney itself it is bewildering excitement even to venture to the streets.' On that day, the papers said, Australia would be celebrating a unique triple event: 'the birth of a New Year, the birth of a new century, and the birth of a new nation'.

On the night of Monday 31 December, the incoming year was greeted by excited crowds — not only in Sydney but in other cities and in scores of lesser centres across the land — sometimes to the accompaniment of clanging firebells and rocket displays, and always with cheers and singing. In some towns a united religious service was held, with psalms, patriotic songs and Auld Lang Syne creating an atmosphere of thanksgiving and of promise for the future.

When the great day dawned newspapers were ready with their expressions of unbounded loyalty, hope, and dedication. Some editors decided to break old rules and celebrate with Commonwealth Day papers printed in patriotic blue. Many devoted their main pages to laudatory reviews of the long struggle to achieve 'a united people', and ran portraits of Governor-General Lord Hopetoun and Lady Hopetoun, flanking the Commonwealth Shield and draped flags.

Sydney's great spectacle in Centennial Park centred around Lord Hopetoun's Proclamation of the Commonwealth. Troops from distant lands as well as from the Australian colonies themselves were drawn up in ceremonial style. There were contingents from India and 1000 men from 'the best English regiments', 300 men from New Zealand (a third of them Boer War veterans), 250 from Tasmania and a 600-man battalion from Victoria (including 100 men just returned from South Africa), and contingents from other colonies. Commemorative arches were set up at key points and Sydney was, in the words of one observer, a city of arches: 'First the arch in Bridge Street, white with wool, bearing in gold letters, "The Land of the Golden Fleece". Then a great, yellow curve, over which wheat and corn make a tender cover as "Ceres Welcomes the New Commonwealth". The French arch next, at the Exchange Corner, low and simple, yellow in colour, and emblazoned with the stirring names of France. Then the American arch, loud, scarlet and ornate, with a great white eagle spreading across it, and bearing greenery in every vacant area. On, up the city . . . the Victorian arch . . . leads to the Commonwealth arch stretching across the street between the city parks, a huge white structure, set out with pictures of our history. And then at Oxford Street the beauty of all the arches, "To Our Comrades of the Southern Sea", the simplest arch of them all, but chaste and touching, with its six white pillars at each end and its straight white lines overhead. This is the last and loveliest on the route, for the coal arch, black, glittering and sombrely imposing, stands away against the green trees in the Domain.'

Tens of thousands of men, women and children, determined to enjoy the pomp and glitter attending the creation of a new nation, lined Melbourne's streets on 9 May 1901 to see the King's son drive on his way to open the national parliament. For the first time a State carriage with traditional postilions and outriders, attendants and footmen, was in use for a Royal occasion. Within the Exhibition Building 12 000 guests were assembled. The *Bulletin*'s social writer was among those who found the spectacle magnificent enough to keep anyone 'interested for a week'. Attention centred on the Duke of Cornwall and York, and the Duchess, who stood at the focal point of the red-carpeted platform. 'Jewels and a white cross sash ("Order Alexandra") enlivened the Duchess' all-black brocaded velvet. The vast floor held an ocean of straining faces which had overflowed the balconies like white foam flung up on cliffs. In the midst of the sea an island of Royal-red, and on this ruddy speck four human figures [the Duke, the Duchess, an equerry, and Madame Nellie Stewart, the prima donna commissioned to sing the new national ode] stood facing . . . Australia's Ministers of State, flanked by State politicians, officials, consuls, soldiers, and sailors, while beyond them a representative mass of ordinary citizens, rich and poor, strained eyes and ears in the endeavour to catch sound or glimpse of this historic ceremony.'

Newspapers and journals went beyond the brilliance of the occasion to point to the importance of the prospect before the new nation. The *Bulletin*'s exuberance was boundless; Australia, an editorial declared, had 'the greatest opportunity which any nation has been blessed with since the writing of the first page of the world's authentic history'. Never before had a continent been 'peacefully united under one government — united by the will of the people, and the people almost wholly of one race and one language'. Abroad, many newspapers and journals acknowledged the new nation's significance, and *The Times* saw the foundation of the Commonwealth as 'one of the chief constitutional events in history'.

For sensitive men and women, nationhood was more than a political development to celebrate; it released profound feelings of national pride. The realisation that the continent was now one Australia, in spirit as well as in name, brought a renewal of faith which encouraged poets to probe the inner meaning of the land, and to find a new field of introspection in its evident

Preceding pages: The Commonwealth of Australia was officially born on 1 January 1901, with the publication of the first issue of the Commonwealth *Gazette,* carrying Queen Victoria's proclamation of the Commonwealth of Australia Constitution Act. The new Australian constitution enabled the six previously independent colonies to federate as States of a national government under a system which incorporated aspects of both the American federation and Westminster government.

Victoria *by the Grace of God of the United Kingdom of Great Britain and Ireland...*

Whereas *...Commonwealth of Australia Cons...*

By the Queen Herself.

Signed with Her own Hand

mysteries and its goodness. John Sandes composed 'An Australian Hymn' (for which Louis Lavater wrote the music) expressing thanks to God for a land stretching

> From jewelled sea to sea,
> From shore to golden shore.

Most of the writers who responded to the challenge of an unplumbed Australia were drawn to the spectral quality of the bush. Thomas Heney saw in it most clearly the awesome nature of a primeval scene with power to overwhelm the puny effort of the individual. Awed by the land's vastness, Heney wrote:

> Hoary are the leagues of bush, and tawny brown its soil;
> In that immensity lost are human effort and toil.

Left: On 9 July 1900, Queen Victoria gave her formal assent to the Commonwealth of Australia Constitution Act of the United Kingdom Parliament. Her Majesty actually signed two copies of the assent; one copy, 'Signed with Her own Hand' (in the upper left-hand corner), together with the pen, inkstand and table she used, she presented to the new Federal Parliament.

Among those ready to seek more positive meanings deep within the Australian heritage were Bernard O'Dowd and Christopher Brennan, two poets of Catholic upbringing who reflected a new wellspring of creative scholarship. Concern for the fragile nature of the land — and a feeling that all might easily be lost to the harsh, materialistic world shaping other destinies — permeated much of what they wrote. This sense of ominous foreboding dominated Brennan's work; O'Dowd shared much the same concern but was generally absorbed with the mystic quality of the land — still 'a prophecy to be fulfilled!' He believed a finer Australia would arise in the future, but he found so much to be savoured that he wanted to preserve the existing goodness. To him, Australia was: 'the Eldorado of old dreamers, the Sleeping Beauty of the world's desire!' He found Australia's distinctive qualities epitomised in the bush, and he built his most introspective and most moving poem on that theme, eulogising 'the great pillared cathedral' as the repository of a goodness Australians should treasure.

Not all shared O'Dowd's deeper and altruistic feelings. The 'world culture' and its standardising influences had emerged to beguile the Western world, and most Australians were firmly in its spell. In pointing to the strength and prospects of the burgeoning nation, the *Southern Spectator* wrote of Australians as 'a thrifty and wealthy people', and gave some of the evidence supporting this materialism. One in three of the entire population had a savings bank account, and the average deposit ran to more than £33, while the general banks held customers' deposits equivalent to £27 for every man, woman, and child in the country. The paid-up capital invested in Australian enterprises was computed to be over £550 000 000, of which British investors had contributed two-thirds and local investors one-third. With all the signs for continued prosperity and progress, the feeling of goodness of life that launched Australians into the 20th century did not fade with the years; rather it grew. Against a changing environment and a quest for speed, men and women clung to the values they treasured. Material standards were high, and well protected; the cluttered parlour and its gramophone, the dining-room's mirrored sideboard with its laden fruit-dish, and the well-stocked wardrobe, promised fulfilment and permanence. In the world at large the rate of change and interchange had speeded up to an unprecedented degree; but as yet there was no real understanding of the growing interdependence, rather a return to the older values. It was a time to cherish the good life — a time for joy and contentment, an Indian Summer for reflection.

Western Australia became independent a decade before the birth of the Commonwealth and celebrated its new status with a series of gold discoveries culminating in the great finds at Coolgardie and Kalgoorlie in 1892-3. Between the towns of Kalgoorlie and Boulder lay one of the world's richest reefs, the fabulous 'Golden Mile'. While eastern Australia was gripped by a depression, the west was launched with a boom. Right: Gold bullion, Kalgoorlie. Opposite page: Mine ruins at Menzies. Below, right: Gold rush buildings, Coolgardie. Over Page: State Hotel, Gwalia.

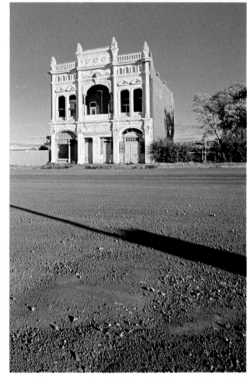

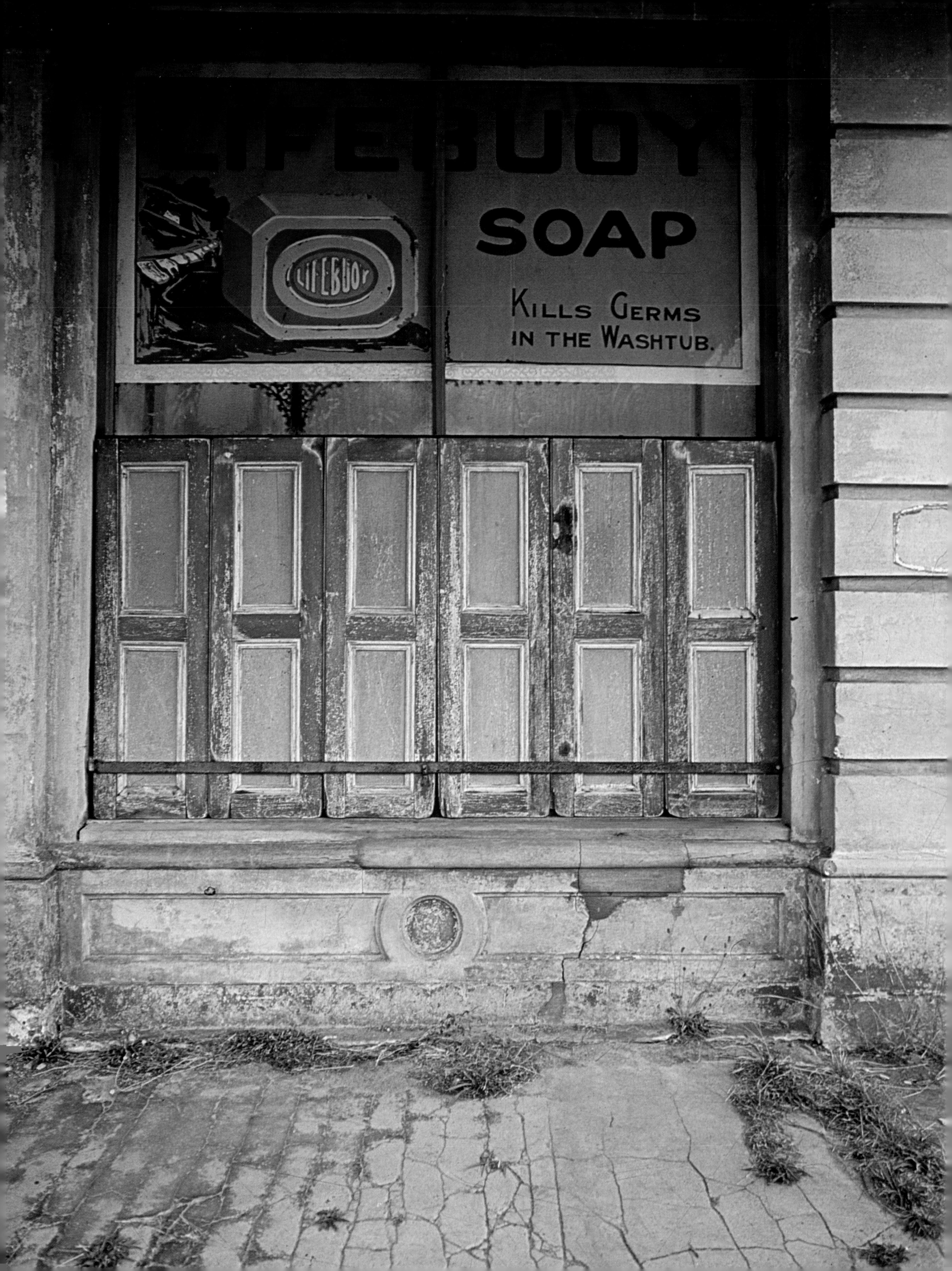
LIFEBUOY
LIFEBUOY
SOAP
KILLS GERMS
IN THE WASHTUB.

Martin Geraghty and his cousin Patrick Brennan built their store in Lennox Street, Maryborough, Queensland in 1871. It sold groceries and their own produce: wines, vinegar and pickles, which they prepared in a three-storey factory they owned nearby. The business was managed by Martin's widow when he died, and on her death by her son George and his sisters. When George Geraghty died in November 1973 his store looked much the same as it had done more than a century earlier. Below, right: Picket fence of store and residence. Below: Carved doorframe of Smellie's warehouse, Brisbane.

Timber and tin were the dominant building materials of the northern settlements and the ingenuity of the vernacular architecture produced numerous methods of providing shade and maximising breezes while at the same time aspiring to decoration. Right: Archer Park railway station, Rockhampton. Left: Park Hotel, Charters Towers. Below: Lattice door screen of Maryborough house. Below, left: Early verandah, Rockhampton.

In the decade before federation there were moves to have Queensland divided into three states: northern, central and southern. Rockhampton, on the north-central coast, was at one time considered to be the likely capital of a new northern state, and its late-nineteenth century architecture matched this aspiration. The Customs House (right), designed by A. B. Brady in classic revival style, was built of Stanwell stone and crowned by a copper-sheathed dome (left). Below, left: Clocktower of the Post Office, 1892. Below: Old Government House, Brisbane, 1862.

In Victorian Australia wealthy men made their homes resplendent with handworked timbers. John Ward, a Brisbane ironmonger, used Queensland hoop pine in the ceiling of 'Auchenflower' (right) which he built in 1876. Part of the house has been re-erected at Earlystreet Village. Thomas Stephens, once owner of the Brisbane *Courier*, built 'Cumbooquepa' (right; left; below) between 1870 and 1890 with fireplaces and bookcases in English oak, cedar and stained pine. Below, left: Library of the Supreme Court, Victoria.

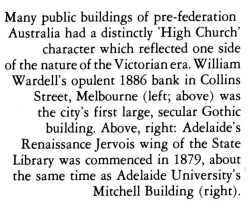

Many public buildings of pre-federation Australia had a distinctly 'High Church' character which reflected one side of the nature of the Victorian era. William Wardell's opulent 1886 bank in Collins Street, Melbourne (left; above) was the city's first large, secular Gothic building. Above, right: Adelaide's Renaissance Jervois wing of the State Library was commenced in 1879, about the same time as Adelaide University's Mitchell Building (right).

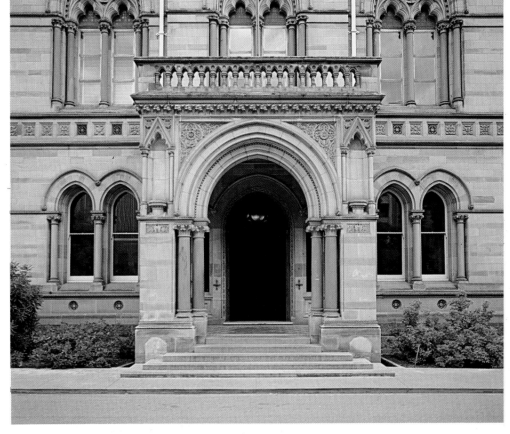

Nymphs and cupids, gods and goddesses and a whole cast of mythological characters in marble and plaster cavorted self-consciously among the populace of the 1880s. While some Australians nourished a vision of a new, young nation about-to-be, others were bent on emulating the glories of bygone ages. Far right: 'The Flight from Pompeii' by Benzoni, Ballarat Botanic Gardens. Above: Ceiling detail, Victorian Legislative Council chamber. Right, above: Carlton Gardens fountain, Melbourne. Right: Princess' Theatre facade, Melbourne.

PRINCESS' THEATRE

The opening of the first federal Parliament took place in Melbourne's Exhibition Building (preceding page) before an invited audience of 12 000 guests on 9 May, 1901. The ceremony concluded with the playing of the 'Hallelujah Chorus', 'Rule Britannia' and the National Anthem. But the jubilation gave way to an air of anti-climax which left Australia's first Governor-General, Lord Hopetoun, £15,000 out of pocket for entertainment, and the new national Parliament without a home for its deliberations. Lord Hopetoun returned to England a poorer man and the parliamentarians took up temporary accommodation in Victoria's State Parliament House (left; above) where they remained for 27 years until a new building was completed in Canberra.

Illustrations

Pages 4-5: 'Endeavour' model constructed by Bruce and Ross Usher, Sydney.

Pages 6-7: Cook's journal by courtesy of the National Library of Australia, Canberra.

Page 12: Facsimile of Dirck Hartog's plate photographed in the Perth Museum, Western Australia.

Pages 14-15: 'Endeavour' model by courtesy of Bruce and Ross Usher.

Page 18: Cook's journal and writing desk in the National Library of Australia, Canberra; Cook's sundial and compass photographed, by permission, in the Mitchell Library, Sydney.

Pages 20-21: The brig 'Perseverance' at the wharf, Old Sydney Town, by courtesy of Old Sydney Town Pty Ltd.

Pages 24, 25: Buildings at Old Sydney Town.

Pages 26, 27: 'Experiment Farm' photographed by courtesy of the National Trust of New South Wales.

Page 32: Victoria Barracks photographed by courtesy of the Commonwealth Department of Defence.

Page 33: Old Government House photographed by courtesy of the National Trust of New South Wales.

Pages 36-37: Sydney Observatory photographed by courtesy of the Commonwealth Department of Science.

Pages 40-41: Photographed with the assistance of Tim Hobson, Curator of History, Sovereign Hill Gold Mining Township, Ballarat, Victoria.

Page 47: Governor's residence, old Darlinghurst Gaol, photographed by courtesy of the New South Wales Department of Education.

Pages 64-65: 'Emu Bottom' homestead photographed by courtesy of Hedley and Jan Elliott.

Page 70: Fauchery's hut photographed at Sovereign Hill Gold Mining Township, Ballarat.

Page 71: Miner's hut from the Tanjil goldfields now reconstructed at the Gippsland Folk Museum, Moe, Victoria. Exterior of Fauchery's hut, Sovereign Hill.

Page 72: Slab hut from Raglan now reconstructed at Sovereign Hill: Cradle of hoop pine photographed at Earlystreet Village, Norman Park, Brisbane.

Page 73: Slab hut at old 'Glenmore' homestead, Rockhampton, photographed by courtesy of the Birbeck family.

Pages 74, 75: 'Emu Bottom' photographed by courtesy of Hedley and Jan Elliott.

Pages 76-79: Governor La Trobe's cottage photographed by permission of the National Trust of Australia (Victoria).

Page 81: Post Office residence interiors photographed at Sovereign Hill.

Page 83: Rhoden's Halfway House photographed by courtesy of the Gippsland Folk Museum, Moe, Victoria.

Page 84: 'Brickendon' outbuilding photographed by courtesy of Mrs. W. F. Archer.

Page 85: Stables at 'Entally' photographed by courtesy of the National Trust of Australia (Tasmania).

Pages 86, 87: 'Strawberry Hill' farm, Albany, photographed by courtesy of the National Trust of Australia (Western Australia).

Pages 88-89: 'Valleyfield' photographed by courtesy of Mr and Mrs J. H. A. Warner.

Pages 90-91: 'Glenrock' photographed by courtesy of Mr Peter Muller.

Pages 92-93: 'Camden Park' photographed by courtesy of Mr and Mrs Quentin Stanham.

Pages 94-95: 'Bedervale' homestead photographed by courtesy of Mr Royal; furniture by courtesy of the National Trust of New South Wales.

Page 96: 'Lanyon' photographed by courtesy of the National Trust of Australia.

Pages 98-99: Gold panning photographed at Sovereign Hill, Ballarat.

Pages 104-106: Photographed at Sovereign Hill.

Pages 108-109: Eureka reconstruction by courtesy of Henry Scott and Neil Speed.

Pages 110-111: Photographed at Sovereign Hill.

Page 112: (lower left) Commercial Bank reconstruction at the Swan Hill Pioneer Settlement; remainder of photography at Sovereign Hill.

Pages 114-123: Photographed at Sovereign Hill.

Page 125: Emu Point Joss House, Bendigo, photographed by courtesy of the National Trust of Australia (Victoria).

Pages 130-131: 'Lake View' photographed by courtesy of the National Trust of Australia (Victoria).

Pages 132-133: Cobb & Co photography at Sovereign Hill.

Pages 136, 137: Cornish miner's cottage, Moonta, photographed by courtesy of the National Trust of South Australia.

Page 148: Burke and Wills' mark at the Menindee Hotel photographed by courtesy of the licensee, Mr Maiden.

Pages 154-155: 'Southampton' station photographed by courtesy of the National Trust of Australia (Western Australia).

Pages 160-161: 'Gulf' station, Yarra Glen, photographed by courtesy of Mr and Mrs D. Fellows.

Page 162: Slab hut photographed by courtesy of Earlystreet Village.

Pages 164-165: 'Glenmore' homestead photographed by courtesy of the Birbeck family.

Pages 166-167: 'Tyntynder' station photographed by courtesy of Mr R. G. Holloway.

Pages 168-171: 'Bungaree' photographed by courtesy of Sir Richard Hawker.

Pages 172-173: 'Para Para' photographed by courtesy of Mr Frank Cook.

Pages 174-175: 'Cordillo Downs' photographed by courtesy of the Beltana Pastoral Company Limited.

Page 176: 'Seppeltsfield' photography by courtesy of B. Seppelt & Sons Limited; 'Yalumba' photographed by courtesy of Mr and Mrs M. Hill-Smith.

Page 180: 'Camden Park' outbuilding photographed by courtesy of Mr and Mrs Quentin Stanham.

Pages 186-187: Old Melbourne gaol photography by courtesy of the National Trust of Australia (Victoria).

Pages 188-189: 'Commonwealth Gazette' photographed by permission of the trustees of the Mitchell Library, Sydney.

Page 192: Queen Victoria's assent photographed by permission of the Speaker of the House of Representatives, Sir Billy Snedden.

Page 194: Gold bullion photographed by courtesy of Gold Mines of Kalgoorlie.

Pages 196-197: State Hotel, Gwalia, photographed by courtesy of Western Mining Corporation.

Page 198: Daydream mine ruins photographed by courtesy of the Broken Hill City Council.

Page 204: Stock Exchange building, Charters Towers, photographed by courtesy of the National Trust of Queensland.

Pages 206-207: Geraghty's store, Maryborough, photographed by courtesy of the National Trust of Queensland.

Page 212: 'Cumbooquepa' study and fireplace photographed by courtesy of Somerville House, Brisbane High School for Girls; Supreme Court Library photographed by permission of the Chief Justice of Victoria.

Page 213: 'Auchenflower' ceiling photographed by courtesy of Earlystreet Village.

Page 214: Gothic banking chamber photographed by courtesy of the ANZ Banking Group Limited.

Page 218: 'Eulalia' photographed by courtesy of Mr Stanley Hancock; 'Ripponlea' by courtesy of the National Trust of Australia (Victoria).